"The two girls grew up at the
edge of the ocean and knew it was
paradise, and better than Eden,
which was only a garden."

—*Eve Babitz*

WILDSAM PURSUITS

*Places are endlessly complex: time, geography, culture and
happenings layered with millions of stories. And often, one realizes
that a place carries a specific heritage, a definitive pursuit that
people build their lives around, a common trade or precious
resource that might set the course for generations.*

For the coast of Southern California, this pursuit is surfing.

WELCOME

EARLY MORNING, ENCINITAS, CALIFORNIA. Sunrise calm blankets the town. Barely anything stirs along the Highway. Tom at Leucadia Donuts unlocks his doors. Lights flick on at Lofty and Ironsmith. The tracks await the Coast Starlight. Farther down, past the old cinema, the gift stores, barrooms and surf shops, a crowd gathers at Swami's. The small parking lot sits on a cliff, what feels like a hundred yards above the beach. Already all but two spots are filled by a menagerie of vehicles. Car doors and hatchbacks stand open, wetsuits and boards sliding out. Light *Hellos, How's it lookings*. Businesslike, even in joy. Before the sun fully emerges into the sky, the first surfers descend the stairs to start another day in the water.

All along this golden coastline, in every town, wherever waves break between San Diego and Santa Barbara, this ritual plays out. It's as trusted as the tides themselves.

Surfing's earliest vibrations reached California from Hawai'i, borne by powerful figures. George Freeth, "the man who walked on water," mesmerized at Redondo. Duke Kahanamoku, one of the great athletes of the last century, carved waves on a mahogany board. But in time, this trans-Pacific import wove itself into the Golden State's DNA. Vice versa, too. In Dana Point, Hobie Alter shaped balsa, then foam and fiberglass; Jack O'Neill stitched wetsuits in his garage. Far more important than the gear, though, California's surfers forged a style. Tom Blake, beach philosopher, could paddle out of 1920s photos straight into a lineup today. Marge Calhoun spent weeks living out of a battered, paneled "surf truck" in the '50s, chasing the biggest waves she could find, adventure personified.

In Southern California, surfing is a community, a way of holding yourself in the world, a sensibility tuned to the ocean's beat. You don't have to surf to catch on. The morning scene at Swami's unfolds right across the way from a meditation center—a SoCal touch, almost too good. But it's true that a bracing alertness fills the air. The tidal pulse radiates out from the sand into Southern California's towns and cities, the breakfast spots and boardwalks—a Cali vibe, chill but ready for the swell.

From early days, surfing acted as an invitation to explore. What's around the next bend of the PCH? Where could an endless summer lead? —The Editors

ESSENTIALS

*Trusted intel and travel info about iconic culture, geography
and entry points to the traditions and landscapes of the
Southern California Coast*

CULTURE

FILM/TV	MUSIC
The Endless Summer	The Beach Boys
Beach Blanket Bingo	Best Coast
Sprout	Little Wings
The OC	Joni Mitchell
Farewell, My Lovely	Chicano Batman
Echo in the Canyon	Jan & Dean
Anchorman	Jackson Browne
The Lincoln Lawyer	Mazzy Star
Baywatch	Kamasi Washington
Santa Barbara	X
Mulholland Drive	Jason Mraz

BOOKS

⌐ *Inherent Vice* by Thomas Pynchon: The mysterious writer's trippy meta-mystery lopes along at a stoned, beach-town pace, its surreal plot quietly charting the disintegration of Cali counterculture idealism.

⌐ *The White Album* by Joan Didion: One of the late essayist's powerful Golden State explorations, definitive on Los Angeles in the 1960s and Malibu's symbolic allure.

⌐ *The Sympathizer* by Viet Thanh Nguyen: A Vietnamese double agent's kaleidoscopic adventures bridge diaspora life and Hollywood's foibles.

⌐ *California Design, 1930-1965: Living in a Modern Way*, edited by Wendy Kaplan: Profusely illustrated companion volume to a LACMA retrospective traces Neutra, Charles and Ray Eames, and a profound style tradition.

⌐ *The House of Broken Angels* by Luis Alberto Urrea: A big riff on family from a novelist with San Diego and Tijuana roots, portraying a Mexican American cancer patient's self-made send-off party.

⌐ *LeRoy Grannis: Surf Photography of the 1960s and 1970s*, edited by Jim Heimann: A doorstop tome befitting an iconic snapper's pictorial legacy.

ISSUES

Erosion | With near-future sea-level rises projected not in inches but in meters, the beaches at the heart of the SoCal mythos are in danger. "Managed retreat," seawalls and sand restoration projects offer some hope, but also challenges in their own right. **EXPERT:** *Charles Lester, director, UC Santa Barbara Ocean and Coastal Policy Center*

Beach Access | By law, anyone can walk on any California beach. In practice, land ownership [and locked gates] can block the way. In 2022, exclusive Hollister Ranch near Santa Barbara began to allow a few visitors onto its storied shores, after years of contention. **EXPERT:** *Susan Jordan, director, California Coastal Protection Network*

Localism | Surfer territorialism is legendary, though protective-ness of "local" breaks has possibly mellowed in recent years with surfing's increased popularity. What has not changed is the need to respect surf etiquette. Paddling straight to the front of the line is never cool, local or not. **EXPERT:** *Jane Schmauss, historian, California Surf Museum*

Algae | It's not the most fun thing to contemplate, but the discharge of sewage from coastal cities breeds harmful ocean algal blooms. Scientists are studying ways to reduce nitrogen levels in the outflow. **EXPERT:** *David Caron, marine scientist, University of Southern California*

STATISTICS

$3.97B .... Estimated value of global surf equipment industry, 2021
375,000 .... Estimated attendance, US Open of Surfing, Huntington Beach
10-15 .... Approx. mountain lion population, Santa Monica Mountains
56 .... U.S. Navy ships based in San Diego
1 .... Rank among busiest U.S. border crossings, San Ysidro Port of Entry
159 .... Registered organic farms, Santa Barbara County

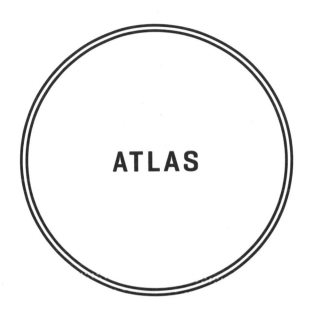

ATLAS

A guide to the lands and places of the Southern California Coast, including curated favorites, communities large and small, and a road trip taking in surf, art and date shakes

LODGING

NEIGHBORHOOD
Palihouse
Santa Barbara
palisociety.com
Palm fronds, stucco,
arched doorways. A
chill enclave near the
Presidio. Lemonade
service a plus.

....

BESPOKE DESIGN
Proper
Santa Monica
properhotel.com
Earthtones.
Mod-classic design
moves. Hit the
beach in 15 minutes.

....

ROADSIDE REDUX
Hotel June Malibu
Malibu
thehoteljune.com
Redone vintage bun-
galows hit a dreamy
Old Malibu stride.

....

MARINA
Lido House
Newport Beach
lidohousehotel.com
Cape Cod aesthetic
meets California
mood. Rooftop bar.

MODERN CABANA
Hotel Joaquin
Laguna Beach
hoteljoaquin.com
All whites and woods.
Cool eye for art and
vintage. Close to
Shaw's Cove.

....

LA HIDEOUT
Hotel Covell
Los Angeles
hotelcovell.com
Refined but homey
retreat, inland, East
Hollywood way.
Cutest wine bar.

....

YURTS AND CABINS
El Capitan Canyon
Santa Barbara
elcapitancanyon.com
Cedar cabins and
campout spirit. Fire-
side astronomy.

....

BEACHHOUSE
Surfrider
Malibu
thesurfrider
malibu.com
A whitewashed
vision slung up in the
chaparral.

SURF RESORT
The Seabird
Oceanside
theseabirdresort.com
Sun-splashed rooms
with serious beach
and palm views. Sea
lettuce vodka in the
bar, FYI.

....

FAMILY FRIENDLY
Terranea
Rancho Palos Verdes
terranea.com
Action stations:
archery, hikes, birds,
whales. Pool on a
dramatic headland.

....

BEACHFRONT
Rosewood Miramar
Montecito
rosewoodhotels.com
True coastal shimmer
in plush surround-
ings. Beachside suites.

....

LEGEND
San Ysidro Ranch
Montecito
sanysidroranch.com
Vine-laced cabins
in the Santa Ynez
Mountains' shadow.

EVENTS

SURF FEST
SurfRodeo
Ventura
July
Blowout wave celebration, with competition and bands on the pier.

....

LGBTQ
Venice Pride
Venice Beach
June
Drag, parades, "Gaywatch" party at historic club Roosterfish.

....

POWWOW
Chumash Day
Malibu
April
Long-running inter-tribal festival. Dance where mountains meet sea.

....

FLEA MARKET
Rose Bowl Flea
Pasadena
Second Sundays
Colossal commerce. A vintage seeker's stadium-sized dream.

FAIR
LA County Fair
Pomona
May
Huge [one of nation's largest] but down-home rendezvous of carnie rides, art and ag.

....

MIGRATION
Festival of the Whales
Dana Point
March
Cali grays bring out the party: clam chowder, ocean excursions.

....

FLOWERS
Coronado Flower Show
San Diego
April
Folksy atmosphere and lavish displays.

....

FOOD FEST
626 Night Market
626nightmarket.com
Summer
Global-cuisine meet-ups across metro LA.

MUSIC FESTIVAL
BeachLife Ranch
Redondo Beach
September
Americana-rooted twin to the spring BeachLife, with big names and proceeds to good works.

....

CAR SHOW
Laguna Beach Car Show
Laguna Beach
October
Hundreds of vintage whips, 1960s Minis to classic woodies.

....

INK FEST
Golden State Tattoo Expo
Pasadena
October
Workshops with top talent.

....

BEER
Tijuana International Beer Festival
Tijuana
June
San Diego and Baja brewers unite.

SHOPPING

For our list of surf shops, see page 72

For our list of surf shops, see page 72

SKATE SHOP
Rip City Skates
1709 Santa Monica Blvd, Santa Monica
Oldest of the old school, with skull logo and Black Flag collabs to prove it.

....

FURNITURE
Garde
1280 Lillie Ave Summerland
Wide-ranging eye for worldly designers, classic and avant. Great lighting and textiles too.

....

MEN'S CLOTHING
Iron & Resin
324 E Main St Ventura
Stronger-than-dirt workwear from a SoCal brand. Shop aprons are a flex.

....

APOTHECARY
Pura Luna
633 Chapala St Santa Barbara
Tinctures, medicinals, vibrations.

WOMEN'S FASHION
Dôen
225 26th St Santa Monica
Hit Brentwood Country Mart for Cali earth energy from two Santa Barbara sisters.

....

MODERN HOME
Nickey Kehoe
7166 Beverly Blvd Los Angeles
Italian tumblers. Barebones garden hoe. Refined finds.

....

INDIE BRANDS
Midland
1404 Micheltorena St Silver Lake
Cali makers: Sugar Candy Mountain, Pietsie, Me & Arrow.

....

JAPANESE GOODS
Tortoise General Store
12701 Venice Blvd Venice
Cool imports for every shelf. The Hakusan cat!

VINYL
Warbler
131 E De La Guerra St, Santa Barbara
New and used. What a record shop should be.

....

VINTAGE HOME
The Blue Door
4 E Yanonali St Santa Barbara
Three wanderable floors of discovery.

....

PLANTS
Botanica
1909 Cable St Ocean Beach
Philodendrons and calatheas for days.

....

BOOKSTORES
D.G. Wills Books
La Jolla
Small World
Venice
Skylight
Los Angeles
Pages
Manhattan Beach
Bart's Books
Ojai
Libélula, Verbatim
San Diego

ART CLASSES
Vita Art Center
Ventura
vitaartcenter.com
Instruction from
mandalas to abstract
landscapes and
ceramics.

....

MURALS
Judy Baca
Los Angeles
sparcinla.org
Since the 1970s,
visionary of *The
Great Wall of Los An-
geles,* an epic visual
history.

....

OUTDOOR CINEMA
Cinespia
Los Angeles
cinespia.org
Screening classics
[*The Birds, But I'm a
Cheerleader*] at iconic
spots around the city.

....

ABSTRACT PAINTER
Sabrina Piersol
San Diego
sabrinapiersol.com
Color explosions,
inspired by nature.

LITERARY JOURNAL
Kaleidoscoped
San Diego
kaleidoscopedmag.com
Platform for wild
word experiments
from the UC San
Diego creative
writing crew.

....

POET LAUREATE
Emma Trelles
Santa Barbara
emmatrelles.com
Capturing nature and
experience in haunt-
ing lines.

....

HANDMADE FLAGS
Slightly Choppy
slightlychoppy.com
Hand-cut letters on
old-time pennants
shout out SoCal's
great surf towns.

....

ART MAGAZINE
East of Borneo
Los Angeles
eastofborneo.org
Heady dive into mod-
ern art, with a strong
American West vibe,
deep online archive.

FILMMAKER
Kevin Jansen
Los Angeles
@robotsfrom
Gritty, cool
explorations of
SoCal surf culture,
including feature
Please Have Fun.

....

SCULPTOR
Woods Davy
Venice
woodsdavy.com
Stones pulled from
the sea combine
into flowing abstract
structures.

....

CERAMICIST
Hana Ward
Los Angeles
hanaward.com
Cute Uno+Uchi
mugs, alongside
serious paintings.

....

FILM FESTIVAL
Santa Barbara
International
sbiff.org
Two big weeks in
spring, Riviera
Theatre all year.

OUTDOORS

LAWN BOWLING
Laguna Beach Lawn
Bowling Club
Laguna Beach
Learn the ways of
the greens with a
free intro lesson.
Members play a
packed schedule.

....

BOTANICAL GARDEN
Lotusland
Montecito
lotusland.org
Fertile dominion
of Madame Ganna
Walska, an all-time
eccentric.

....

DAY HIKE
Tangerine Falls
Los Padres
National Forest
A seasonal gusher,
just a rugged mile up
Cold Creek Canyon.

....

SOCCER
Venice Beach FC
Venice
venicebeachfc.com
Famed pickup battles
on the hard courts of
Estadio de Dogtown.

SKI AREA
Mount Baldy
San Gabriel Mtns
mtbaldyresort.com
Surf in the morning,
ski in the afternoon:
SoCal snow, just 90
minutes from Hun-
tington Beach.

....

BEACH VOLLEYBALL
Huntington
Beach Pier
surfcityusa.com
Many courts, all
levels daily, pro tour
Open in November.

....

FISHING TRIPS
Helgren's
Oceanside
helgrensportfishing.com
Daily outings with
veteran anglers,
quarry changing with
the seasons.

....

RUNNING
Run North County
San Diego
runnorthcounty.com
Welcoming group
outings just about
daily, many levels.

CYCLING ROUTE
Ventura River
Parkway Trail
Ventura County
Roll the 16.5 miles
from the ocean to
Ojai on a smooth
rail-to-trail setup.

....

KAYAK
LA River
Expeditions
Los Angeles
lariverexpeditions.org
Paddling near Dodger
Stadium? It's true.

....

THRU-HIKE
Trans-Catalina Trail
Catalina Island
A remote trek
through the island
interior, with 10,000
feet of elevation gain
and fox sightings.

....

SKATEBOARDING
Venice Skatepark
Venice
veniceskatepark.com
Rip through
vast bowls on the
sand stretch where
legends were made.

EXPERTS

INDIGENOUS CULTURE
Julie Tumamait-
Stenslie
bvbmi.com
Chumash elder and
tribal chair, steeped
in history and cur-
rent issues.

....

GUITARS
Tomás Delgado
candelas.com
Third-generation
maker of six-strings
for classical and
flamenco. [Kim Deal
has one too.]

....

CLEAN WATER
Tracy Quinn
healthebay.org
Heads org that works
to protect Santa
Monica Bay and
posts daily beach
condition updates.

....

TATTOOS
Kari Barba
outerlimitstattoo.com
Intense artist of
blacks and grays, often
riffing on maritime
themes.

VINTAGE GEAR
Rewind Audio
rewindaudio.com
LA source for
throwback speakers,
turntables and amps.
Rentals dress up
many film sets.

....

CONDORS
Estelle Sandhaus
@esandhaus
Santa Barbara
Zoo conservation
director helps the
majestic birds regain
SoCal coastal skies.

....

GRASSLANDS
Justin Luong
justinluong.com
Ecologist studying
the effects of drought
on native fields, mak-
ing Pride flags out of
wildflowers.

....

ANIMAL MIGRATION
Clark Stevens
clarkstevens.com
Architect of a land-
mark bridge to help
cougars cross a Santa
Monica freeway.

TINNED FISH
Fishwife
eatfishwife.com
Sustainably sourced
seafood, West Coast
and beyond, with
artful branding and
smart recipes online.

....

ESSAYIST
Rosecrans Baldwin
rosecransbaldwin.com
Wide-ranging LA
study *Everything Now*
brings a little of that
clear-eyed Didion
magic to today's city.

....

LINGUISTICS
Pamela Munro
ucla.edu
Decades of work
with Native
American languages
inform efforts to
revive Tongva.

....

SPORTS
Selema Masekela
@selema
Co-creator of epic
book *Afrosurf*,
founder of Stoked
program for kids.

CITIES & TOWNS

*All along the coast, charming beach towns blend with major cities
to form a global village, gazing to the Pacific horizon.*

SAN DIEGO

"Only a few years ago Balboa Park ... was a barren waste of mesa land," proclaimed an official 1925 guide. Horticulturist Kate Sessions reshaped the expanse for the Panama-California Exposition in 1915, and now its Spanish architecture houses a parade of museums. A priority: THE MUSEUM OF PHOTOGRAPHIC ARTS. The San Diego Zoo, a worldwide conservation icon, sprawls across 100 acres. After all that walking, post up at one of this craft capital's many breweries. Newer taprooms like AMPLIFIED ALE WORKS or Latina-owned MUJERES BREW HOUSE sit near the Marina District's Pacific-chic steakhouse Animae, featuring Tara Monsod's pan-Asian menu. And you've seen the pictures, but landmark HOTEL DEL CORONADO is worth a real-life visit, at least a drink on the Sun Deck.

SURF WATCH	
Sunset Cliffs	POPULATION: 1.38 million
Postcard-perfect perch	COFFEE: Dark Horse
on Point Loma	BEST DAY OF THE YEAR: Comic-Con International, July

LA JOLLA & BIRD ROCK

It would be easy to write off La Jolla and Bird Rock as chichi beach 'burbs. But sit down with a copy of local daily the *La Jolla Light* and a pistachio strawberry croissant at WAYFARER BREAD & PASTRY, and a tight-knit community with endearing, storied layers unfolds. In La Jolla Village proper, D.G. WILLS BOOKS looks like a trading post from an old Western. Peruse the outdoor shelves while you wait for your turn to browse the deep stacks inside. The LA JOLLA RECREATION CENTER stands as a monument to newspaperwoman Ellen Browning Scripps, who commissioned architect Irving Gill for its design in 1915. If hitting the courts or the pool isn't the move, keep walking to the MUSEUM OF CONTEMPORARY ART SAN DIEGO, where Scripps' famed home is part of a newly renovated complex.

LIBRARY	
Athenaeum Music & Arts Library	POPULATION: 38,261
Genre-specific collection	COFFEE: The Flower Pot Cafe and Bakery
and studio classes	BEST DAY OF THE YEAR: When the wind's coming from the W/NW

LAGUNA BEACH

Known as safe harbor for surfers and artists, this south Orange Country seaside town is a place where past and present float together. ORANGE INN has served roadside breakfasts to travelers and field hands since 1931. ZINC CAFE & MARKET has a more Nancy Meyers-directed aesthetic, with the avocado toast and its confetti of sliced radish, dill and chives as the real star. The old-school and the now meet at LAGUNA BEACH HOUSE, a hotel steeped in surf culture and local art. Creativity maintains a stronghold here, from the Laguna Art Museum to LAGUNA COLLEGE OF ART AND DESIGN. For a free, year-round visual showstopper of a different kind, spend early evening at bougainvillea- and ice-plant-draped Heisler Park. And finally, the standing advice for burrito recs? Ask the folks at any surf shop. They'll know.

RECORD SHOP	POPULATION: 22,795
Sound Spectrum	COFFEE: The Greeter's Corner
Jim Otto opened shop in '67,	BEST DAY OF THE YEAR:
with Monterey Pop inspiration	Sawdust Art Festival, Jun-Aug

NEWPORT BEACH & BALBOA ISLAND

The oft-quoted line "There's always money in the banana stand" from TV series *Arrested Development* has real ties to Balboa Island's Marine Avenue: SUGAR 'N' SPICE, a snack spot specializing in frozen bananas dredged in chocolate on a stick, inspired the fictional Bluth business. The stand is a fixture on this idyllic main drag, alongside dollar-bill-wallpapered CROCKER'S [have an Island Frank] and beloved breakfast spot WILMA'S PATIO. Off the harbor-enveloped edges of the man-made isle, Newport Beach, a hideaway for Old Hollywood stars of yore, has its classics, too, like THE CRAB COOKER for clam chowder, housemade bread and softshells. Lido Marina Village, an ivory-walled compound with national names like Clare V., Le Labo, Faherty, and Nobu, brings in the new. Indie shop LIDO VILLAGE BOOKS, long part of the boardwalk scene, remains a literary lighthouse.

BOTANICA	POPULATION: 87,502 [combined]
Sherman Library and Gardens	COFFEE: Huskins
Oasis with horticultural	BEST DAY OF THE YEAR:
archives and art	Wooden Boat Festival, June

LONG BEACH

Before it was one of California's largest cities, Long Beach was the site of many Tongva settlements along coast and river. Through a winding history as resort, factory town, and oil center, it became one of the world's biggest ports. Today, it's notable for big events like April's GRAND PRIX OF LONG BEACH, a mammoth pro street race, and July's LONG BEACH PRIDE FESTIVAL AND PARADE, which draws over 80,000 attendees. But the gems come at smaller scale too, via the smart selections at Bel Canto Books or the celebrated ribs of ROBERT EARL'S BBQ. Harbor Breeze Cruises gets out on the water; Rosie's Dog Beach provides a 4-acre oasis for the four-legged. Just south, in Seal Beach, HARBOUR SURFBOARDS has kept on shaping rides since 1959.

GARDEN STOP	POPULATION: 456,062
Earl Burns Miller Japanese Garden	COFFEE: Recreational
Lush 1-acre respite	BEST DAY OF THE YEAR: Catalina Ski Race, July

VENICE

Venice began as a millionaire's dreamy homage to the Italian city of canals and bridges, plotted out by Abbot Kinney as a resort destination before Greater Los Angeles absorbed it. It became a place where waves of subculture wash ashore—Dogtown skaters, streetside artisans, Muscle Beach. Cali lifestyles converge at CAFÉ GRATITUDE, where the modernist vegan fare includes a tofu banh mi called "I Am Charismatic." This is home turf for GARRETT LEIGHT, maker of instant-Cali-cool sunglasses, and Gjelina, one of the defining California restaurants of recent years. And the creative scene remains distinct, palpable at the studio of sculptor ELIZABETH ORLEANS and the adventurous Venice Institute of Contemporary Art. As the day comes to a close, if luck holds, you'll be watching pods of dolphins parade the bay from the VENICE V HOTEL.

SUB SANDWICHES	POPULATION: 27,556
Bay Cities Italian Deli	COFFEE: Groundwork
Utah, get me two!	BEST DAY OF THE YEAR: Pier 360 Beach Sports & Summer Festival, June

MONTECITO & CARPINTERIA

To take a straight dose of Montecito, a plush Santa Barbara suburb, hit MONTECITO COUNTRY MART, a breezy architectural throwback to the 1960s and home to a lot of very now brands. [Clare V., Clic, Hudson Grace, and whatever you do, don't skip RORI'S ice cream.] BETTINA, nestled here like a dashing Italian exchange student, rounds it all out with pizza and negronis. The road down the coast winds through Summerland, home to fine shops like The Well [vintage, garden] and Porch [art, textiles]. In nearby Carpinteria, the SEAL SANCTUARY shows off fin-footed denizens lolling on the sand below. The classic next move is THE SPOT, famous for its as onion rings and creamy milkshakes. On the more upscale side of things, head up picturesque Linden Avenue to LITTLE DOM'S SEAFOOD for oysters and amaretto sours.

BREAKFAST STOP	POPULATION: 27,472 [TOTAL]
Tacos To Go	COFFEE: Lucky Llama
Chile verde burritos [inside Beach Liquor]	BEST DAY OF THE YEAR: Avocado Festival, October

VENTURA

Once you're ready to step away from the beaches [Surfer's Point for the athletic; Emma Wood for wildlife spotting; SAN BUENAVENTURA for immediate access from downtown], this laid-back waterfront town offers plenty more. Excellent Mexican spots line Ventura Avenue, including local icon JOHNNY'S MEXICAN FOOD and takeout-only hole-in-the-wall LALO'S FAST FOOD. Stroll through downtown to find a steal at a thrift store, and stop in at Findings Market for locally designed clothes, footwear and homegoods. Then do as the locals do and enjoy a beer in the sunshine at one of many homegrown breweries—like the Ojai Pixie IPA, tangy with local tangerines, at TOPA TOPA, or the grapefruit-forward Eyegaze Hazy IPA at MADEWEST.

PUTT-PUTT STOP	POPULATION: 114,473
Golf N' Stuff	COFFEE: Kay's Coffee Shop
Navigate the Mystic Castle	BEST DAY OF THE YEAR: Ventura County Fair, August

ENCINITAS

An archetypal surf town hugging Highway 101, Encinitas still has a scruffy vibe, a magnet for those who want to live among the swells. Take it in at SWAMI'S, the main surf break where riders gather at dawn, or watch from the park at the top of the bluff near the local ashram that gives these waves their cheeky name. SALT CULTURE, owned by Sophie and pro-surfer husband Rob Machado, stirs a beach breeze of women's fashion and surf gear. A swing north hits LEUCADIA DONUT SHOPPE, where Tom and Emily Cheu have been frying dough and pouring kona coffee for more than 30 years. LA PALOMA THEATRE, an early spot for 1920s "talkies" and, later, live shows by the likes of Ralph Stanley, sometimes puts classic surf movies on the screen. And keeping up the culture beat, Lou's Records has drawn vinyl hunters since the 1980s.

HAPPY HOUR	POPULATION: 61,762
Le Papagayo	COFFEE: Ironsmith
Full-package 101 experience:	BEST DAY OF THE YEAR:
tacos, sangria, live music	Wavecrest woodies car show, September

SANTA BARBARA

In the mind's eye, Santa Barbara is a land of sun, surf, natural beauty and cultural crunch, thanks to UC Santa Barbara's 20,000-plus students. Checks out! Vibrant surf culture fuels shops like TRIM and Surf Country; in the hills, the hike up RATTLESNAKE CANYON reveals epic city views. Back in town, SB's food scene is arguably undersung. At BIBI JI, an innovative Indian menu plays nice with a natural wine list by lauded somm Rajat Parr. For a pure California high note, head for Satellite, home of the tower of vegan power known as the "YOGA PANTS SALAD." A core area of Santa Barbara's heart is known as THE FUNK ZONE. And yes, the name is ... concerning. But the Zone is where Santa Barbarians of all stripes enjoy galleries, people-watching and local craft drinks. Try RINCON BREWERY. This place is all you hoped it'd be.

SWEET SPOT	POPULATION: 88,255
McConnell's Fine Ice Creams	COFFEE: Handlebar
West Coast dream scoop: Eureka lemon,	BEST DAY OF THE YEAR:
Willamette Valley marionberries	Old Spanish Days, August

ROAD TRIP

*An adventure along the ocean's edge leads through mellow towns,
art and culture centers, island times and a plunge into the waves.*

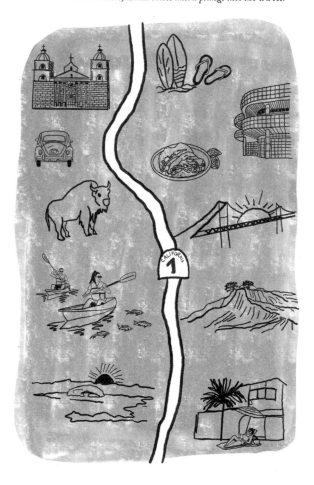

NORTH COUNTY BEACH TOWNS

Gather the good vibrations while meandering north of San Diego through the epitome of SoCal: a garland of laid-back communities.

BIRD ROCK Originally named Bird Rock, City by the Sea, in 1906. Founded a century later, Bird Rock Coffee Roasters, one of the area's first shops to brew single-origin beans, has found a solid community foothold. Just across the street, dreamily design-minded Hermosa Surf serves up smoothies and hand-shapes boards.

LA JOLLA While La Jolla Cove is more than fine to admire from above on the sidewalk, the even-occasionally-adventurous should behold it from a sea kayak. La Jolla Sea Cave Kayaks' guides take paddlers into the marine protected area's arches and cliffs, where leopard sharks and rays float beneath.

TORREY PINES Home to serious research outfits like the Salk Institute, which looks into cures for cancer, and the University of California, San Diego, a big marine biology school. As, perhaps, a contrast in formality, Black's Beach, a notoriously difficult-to-reach part of the shoreline, has a reputation as one of the state's few remaining clothing-optional beaches.

CARDIFF Sure, Cardiff offers plenty of spots within view of the waves, like longtime Mexican staple Las Olas and Zumbar Coffee & Tea. But a picnic is the way to go, with indie grocery Cardiff Seaside Market just steps from San Elijo State Beach.

ENCINITAS Encinitas-born brothers Nikki and Sander Harth recently renovated an old eight-room motel into Surfhouse Boutique Hotel, so visitors could stay awhile in their hometown. Wake up and walk down to Tom and Emily Cheu's Leucadia Donut Shoppe. And stop for DIY art landmarks the Surfing Madonna mural and Dave's Rock Garden on the way to Moonlight Beach.

CARLSBAD In March, more than 50 acres of frilly, ruffled ranunculus begin to bloom in sunset shades of pink, orange, red and yellow at The Flower Fields, exemplar of the area's place in flower farming. Campfire's wood-fueled hearth and Jeune et Jolie get frequent favorite mentions from San Diegans, despite their 35-mile distance from the city proper.

FISH TACOS AND DATE SHAKES

Two Southern California icons make for an ideal hot eat/cool treat combo. Make multiple stops in the name of research.

Between the desert's groves of date palms and the Pacific's bounty, two foodway traditions took hold along the coast: fish tacos and the date shake. At PEDRO'S in San Clemente, a post-surf-snack mainstay since 1986, fish filets are breaded and fried [Baja-style], then folded up with slaw, pico and crema-style dressing. For dessert, go steady with the date shake at CRYSTAL COVE SHAKE SHACK, a cheerful yellow walk-up spot [no relation to the major chain]. Although smoothie versions can hit the spot, this one is a true shake, thick with vanilla ice cream and chunky bits of crystalline date. Let the sugar rush over you while watching the waves lap against the state park below—a near-perfect vintage postcard in real life.

TACOS	SHAKES
El Pescador Fish Market	Orange Inn
La Jolla	*Laguna Beach*
The Taco Stand	Swami's Cafe
Encinitas	*Encinitas*
Oscars Mexican Seafood	Cafe Vida
North Pacific Beach	*Culver City*
City Tacos	John's Garden
Encinitas	*Malibu*

LA COUNTY'S COASTAL MUSEUMS

A cultural cavalcade unfolds along the southern coast between Long Beach and Malibu.

MUSEUM OF LATIN AMERICAN ART [MOLAA]

Begin in Long Beach with an astounding collection of over 1,300 permanent works and a 15,000-square-foot sculpture garden from Latin American artists like Darío Escobar, Liliana Porter, Laura Aguilar and Frida Kahlo. New exhibitions spotlight global talent.

....

MUSEUM OF FLYING

Hug the curves around the Palos Verdes Peninsula on Palos Verdes Drive to this delightfully geeky trove in Santa Monica: a jet-flight simulator, historic aircrafts. Home to California's Aviation Hall of Fame.

....

GETTY CENTER

Funny how culture works sometimes: a midcentury oil tycoon's fortune ended up remaking LA's art-world identity. Perched on a hill over the city's Brentwood neighborhood, this free flagship features stunning architecture, gardens and rotating exhibits focusing on pre-20th-century artwork as well as photographs from the 1800s to present. One moment: the stark form of Italian sculptor Giacomo Manzù's *Cardinale Seduto* against Cali-blue skies on the South Terrace.

....

GETTY VILLA MUSEUM

Hop on the PCH and climb a steep cliff to this extravagant vision of statues, artifacts, and a large reflecting pool. The replica ancient villa's views of the Pacific amplify the Mediterranean mood.

....

FREDERICK R. WEISMAN MUSEUM OF ART

A short drive to Malibu on the PCH takes you to this Pepperdine University hub of contemporary and historical art, which focuses on California as a formative aesthetic influence. Past exhibits have included Andy Warhol, Rodin and selections from the Kinsey African American Art & History Collection.

You can't see the ocean from there, but the Los Angeles County Museum of Art [LACMA] *is a cultural must.*

CATALINA ISLAND DAY TRIP

DAY 4

A ferry ride from the mainland takes you to the California islands, and a very different outlook on the Golden State.

Make the 6 a.m. passage on the CATALINA EXPRESS to Avalon, a far-flung island town of 4,000. Look out for whales, dolphins and seabirds as the light unfurls. Once onshore, fuel for the day at the CATALINA COFFEE AND COOKIE CO., noted for breakfast burritos. Snag a spot on the Catalina Island Company's popular Bison Expedition to see the free-ranging herd originally brought here in the 1920s for *The Vanishing American*, a Western film based on a novel by Zane Grey. [No worries, it's all at a safe distance.] A private cabana at the DESCANSO BEACH CLUB hints at an island life anyone could get used to. Gaze out at mainland California, linger over a fruit smoothie, hop in the turquoise water. You're here and nowhere else, that's for sure. If one day doesn't quite satisfy the Catalina allure, HOTEL ATWATER is a century-old haunt with deco flair. Or trek to the Hermit Gulch Campground, first stop on the Trans-Catalina Trail, a 38.5-mile thru-hike that traverses the island and offers exceptional beach camping. If come evening it's time to get back to mainland reality, catch the last ferry to Long Beach.

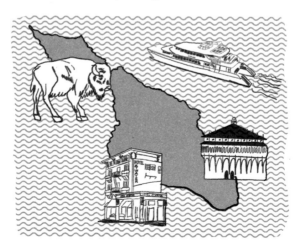

<table>
<tr><td>

DAY
5

</td><td>

SANTA BARBARA
End your coastal journey in a city that defines
Southern California's sunny charms.

</td></tr>
</table>

EARLY
MORNING

How to start your last day on the Southern California
coast? Easy: Surfing. Beginners should check out the small
breaks at LEADBETTER or CAMPUS POINT. Confident surfers should try REFUGIO or EL CAPITÁN. Experts—and their
spectators—can head to TARANTULA'S or JALAMA BEACH.
Any and all can outfit at Channel Islands' flagship shop.

BREAKFAST

Sate your post-surf appetite with a breakfast burrito at
LITO'S MEXICAN RESTAURANT. Lito's is the real deal: a
family-run institution with homemade salsa and a warm,
no-frills atmosphere. Vegetarians, try the nopales [cactus]
and egg; meat eaters, go for the machaca or chorizo. And
don't forget one of each salsa: red, green, and tomatillo.

AFTERNOON

Resist the urge to nap. Instead, digest as you stroll through
Santa Barbara's history. Your choice: Either walk be-
neath the bell towers and arches of OLD MISSION SANTA
BARBARA, dating to 1786 and often called the "Queen of the
Missions." Or head to the huge SANTA BARBARA BOTANIC
GARDEN, designed with over 1,000 species of entirely indig-
enous plants, including the distinctive peeling red bark of
the manzanita trees and the explosive fuchsia of the beaver-
tail cactus. With enough coffee, you can even hit both spots.
[The mission closes at 4 p.m., the gardens at 5.]

EVENING

Find your finale by driving north along Highway 154 West
to COLD SPRING TAVERN. It's only 15 miles from downtown,
but it feels a world away. Tucked in a shady canyon, the tavern is virtually unchanged since its time as a stagecoach stop
in the 1800s. [And, in fact, it's only changed ownership twice
since then.] Now it's a favorite of bikers passing through for
live music from local bands. On weekends, seek the coveted
tri-tip barbecue outside; otherwise, get a bowl of chili [wild
game black bean or the house special] and a cold beer from
the Log Cabin Bar. Grab a picnic table under the trees, and
enjoy the very SoCal scene.

MORE THAN 25 ENTRIES ⟿

ALMANAC

----

*A deep dive into the cultural heritage of
the Southern California Coast through news clippings,
timelines, writings and other historical hearsay*

VENICE

The dream of speculator Abbot Kinney, Venice, future home to skaters and musclemen, was conceived as a watery echo of its Italian counterpart.

VENICE: THE PLAYGROUND OF AMERICA
[Promotional flier, circa 1920]

The Canals of Venice were excavated in 1905 and donated to the city by Mr. Kinney in 1912. There are three miles of these beautiful waterways traversing the choicest residential section of the city. Their banks are lined with flowers and arched with unique bridges and each canal is illuminated at night with a different color scheme. Boating and canoeing in these artistic surroundings are ideal and all kinds of pleasure crafts are to be had at a reasonable rental at the Boathouse on the lagoon. Ocean water is supplied through a channel, connecting with the Pacific at Playa Del Ray.

SPANISH MISSIONARIES

Letter from Junípero Serra, 1769

"We have seen Indians in immense numbers, and all those on this coast of the Pacific contrive to make a good subsistence on various seeds, and by fishing. The latter they carry on by means of rafts or canoes, made of tule [bullrush] with which they go a great way to sea. They are very civil. All the males, old and young, go naked; the women, however, and the female children, are decently covered from their breasts downward. We found on our journey, as well as in the place where we stopped, that they treated us with as much confidence and good-will as if they had known us all their lives. But when we offered them any of our victuals, they always refused them. All they cared for was cloth, and only for something of this sort would they exchange their fish or whatever else they had."

Colonialism devastated California's Indigenous peoples. Estimates hold that the population around San Juan Capistrano, for example, dropped 74 percent between 1770 and 1830. Today's Juaneño Band of Mission Indians maintains a history of the Acjachemen Nation at jbmian.com.

SURFERS OF NOTE

MIKI DORA A.k.a. "Da Cat," "The Black Knight," "The Fiasco Kid," many other nicknames. Acknowledged kingpin of early Malibu scene. Legendary on the longboard. Notoriuous for attitude, international scams and [more seriously] racist statements and beliefs. Died 2002, still a hot-button subject.

LANCE CARSON One of the best when Malibu stood center stage, 1960s. Relaxed style led to suggestion in the film *The Endless Summer* that Carson could eat a ham sandwich while noseriding.

JOYCE HOFFMAN Longboard-era star. Two world titles, 1965 and 1966. Shortboarding's rise around 1970 ended her dominance; she switched to auto racing.

MARGO OBERG A stand-out on the singlefins of the shortboard revolution; won the first women's pro world title in 1977. Catch her in *Five Summer Stories*.

TOM CURREN One of shortboarding's foremost stylists. Won three world titles between 1985 and 1990. Smooth yet powerful: an enduring standard. Enigmatic. Subject of 1997 documentary *Searching for Tom Curren*.

LISA ANDERSEN Four-time world champion, a.k.a. "Trouble," ran away from Florida to California to become a pro surfer. Mixed slashing power with girl-next-door appearance. Subject of 2019 documentary *Trouble*.

JOEL TUDOR Two-time longboard champ from Del Mar, known for seamless flow, noseriding ease, outspoken opinions.

KASSIA MEADOR Malibu regular, stylish noserider at the longboard revival's forefront. Also a photographer and owner of women's wetsuit brand Kassia.

DANE REYNOLDS Lofts huge airs and carves massive, radical turns. Ranked fourth in the world in 2010. Widely considered the best shortboard free surfer of his generation.

RYAN BURCH When his shortboard sponsor wouldn't make him a longboard, Burch made his own. Can ride just about anything.

CAITY SIMMERS Multitalented Oceanside local, part of women shortboard contingent pushing boundaries with next-level aerials, powerful turns and skilled barrel-riding. In 2021, she won the US Open at Huntington Beach.

POP ARCHITECTURE

In the early days of roadside culture, California drivers could spot oversized coffee pots or doughnuts—buildings advertising products in the most literal way. Often called "pop," "programmatic" or "mimetic architecture"—even "duck buildings"—its heyday ran from the 1920s through the '60s.

TOED INN *Santa Monica, 1920s* Frog-shaped, with turned-in toes, this restaurant first loomed in Santa Monica; moved to Wilshire Boulevard after 1938 flood damage.

SANDERSON HOSIERY *West Los Angeles, 1949* A 30-foot leg outside a hosiery factory, reminiscent of the lamp from *A Christmas Story* [though in nude nylons, not fishnets].

PUP CAFÉ *Culver City, 1920s* Diners could enter this restaurant by walking under the chin of a droopy-eyed pup, with chili hot dogs and burgers waiting for them inside.

WILSHIRE COFFEE POT *Los Angeles, 1920s* This circular walk-up served Ben-Hur brand coffee from underneath a giant, gleaming pot with handle and spout.

THE BROWN DERBY *Los Angeles, 1926* Shaped like a derby hat, the restaurant became an emblem for Hollywood's golden age. Domed structure still survives as part of a Wilshire Boulevard shopping center.

THE CREAM CAN *Los Angeles, 1920s* Stools lined the open-air perimeter of an oversized cream can that served all things dairy—ice cream, shakes, buttermilk, cottage cheese.

TONY'S TRANSMISSION *Los Angeles, 1960s* Classic example of a "muffler man," oversized characters made of fiberglass, which could hold an object as advertisement.

LA SALSA MAN *Malibu, 1960s* Twenty-plus feet tall, this muffler man originally presided over a Frostie Freeze while holding a burger. He stands on, with mustache, sombrero and serape.

BIG DONUT DRIVE-IN/RANDY'S DONUTS *Inglewood, 1953* Renamed Randy's from its original moniker, star of many music videos and films.

Jim Heimann's 2018 book California Crazy *charts the history [and whimsy] of the architectural phenomenon.*

BRUCE'S BEACH

Willa and Charles Bruce faced racist backlash from their white neighbors in Manhattan Beach when they bought a seaside parcel of land in 1912 and turned it into a Black beach resort. They called it Bruce's Beach, and it became a lively oasis with a bathhouse, restaurant and dancehall just steps from the ocean. But in the 1920s, the city seized the property and other nearby Black-owned parcels under eminent domain, ostensibly to build a public park. By 1927, all of the resort's structures had been destroyed. Yet the land sat vacant for decades before it finally became a park in the 1960s. It wasn't until 2007 that the park was renamed "Bruce's Beach," but even then its true history went unacknowledged. In 2021, following a successful campaign by an advocacy group led by community organizer Kavon Ward, Governor Gavin Newsom signed into law a bill returning the land to the descendants of Charles and Willa Bruce—a move hailed as the first of its kind, and a potential model for future restorations.

GIDGET

Frederick Kohner seems an unlikely icon of surfing culture: born in Austria-Hungary in 1905, he joined the Jewish and intellectual exodus from Nazi Germany. But in 1957, he published a novel inspired by his daughter Kathy's surf-world adventures. Adapted to film, and later TV, Gidget boosted the pastime's popularity to heights previously unknown. A snippet:

You say "Malibu" and immediately you think of the movie colony and the snazzy beach houses—and James Mason wading into the sundown on account of being a has-been and all. That's not the Malibu I'm writing about. What I mean is that one small bay along the twenty-seven miles of Rancho Malibu right next to the pier where the waves from Japan crash against the shore like some bitchen rocket bombs. ... When you graduate from Malibu you move down to San Onofre or Tressle where the real big humps come blasting in.

In 2021, Kathy Kohner-Zuckerman, aged 80, told Vanity Fair: *"I am the girl that surfed. I am the daughter of Frederick Kohner, who wrote a wonderful story. I am not a movie actress, I am not an influencer. ... I enjoy it. I'm pretty amazed; I lived it all."*

AVOCADOS

Annual Report, California Avocado Association, 1915

A person of ingenuity can find many delicious ways of serving the avocado. There are many varieties of avocados, and they vary very considerably in flavor and texture. Be careful to buy good-quality fruit, free from fiber and not too ripe. Learn to identify good varieties. The fruit can be purchased hard and ripened at home, the same as the Bartlett pear. It is ready for eating when it yields to the slight pressure of the thumb. The flesh is about the consistency of well-made butter, if the fruit is ripe. An unripe avocado is of small charm to the palate, but a ripe one lives long in the memory of delicious flavors.

AVOCADO SERVED IN SKIN Cut the fruit in half. Carefully remove the seed. Serve a half to each person with any of the following dressings, as personal taste directs: 1. Lemon or lime juice. 2. Salt. 3. Sugar. 4. Tomato catsup. 5. Mayonnaise. 6. French dressing.

AVOCADO ON TOAST Remove the flesh with a spoon and mash with a fork. Spread thickly on a small square of hot toast. Add a little salt and pepper. This is one of the nicest ways of serving avocado.

AVOCADO WITH CAVIAR Prepare as the above recipes direct. Spread a small quantity of caviar on top of each piece. This is a very delicious appetizer.

SELECTED CITRUS

MANDARINQUAT
What you think: kumquat/ mandarin crossbreed. Tart delight.

TAROCCO BLOOD ORANGE
An Italian favorite. Needs some chilly nights.

IMPROVED MEYER LEMON
Gardeners' go-to for aromatic blossoms, ample fruit.

WASHINGTON NAVEL ORANGE
Easy peeler, maybe California's first-choice orange.

CARA CARA ORANGE
Sassy Venezuelan import with rosy pink flesh.

BEARSS LIME
Cali's most popular lime. Evergreen, ever-fruiting.

HOBIE ALTER

Milestones of a surf pioneer.

EARLY 1950s Teenage Hobie begins shaping balsa boards in family's summerhouse garage in Laguna Beach.

1953 Alter's father, tired of wood shaving mess, buys him a lot on the Pacific Coast Highway for $1,500.

1954 Hobie Surf Shop opens. Reckoned the first surf shop in Southern California.

1958 Alter and Gordon "Grubby" Clark begin experimenting with surfboards made of fiberglass and foam.

1961 Alter sells surfboards in a booth at an Anaheim boat show next to Art Javes, designer of the Aqua Cat sailboat. Inspired, Alter turns his focus to the catamaran with Hobie Cat Company.

1968 Alter creates the Hobie Cat, a design similar to Aqua Cat but more readily beached. The company goes on to develop more than 20 sailing and watercraft products.

2011 Alter inducted into the National Sailing Hall of Fame before dying of cancer three years later.

INDIGENOUS PEOPLES

Some of the oldest human remains ever discovered in North America came to light in Southern California: Santa Rosa Island's 13,000-year-old Arlington Springs Man. At the time of European contact in the 1700s, nearly 300,000 Indigenous people, speaking more than 135 languages, occupied today's state. Southern California includes homelands of the Chumash, Serrano, Alliklik, Kitanemuk, Gabrielino-Tongva, Kumeyaay and others. Today there are more than 100 federally recognized tribes in the state, and many not yet federally recognized. It is estimated that Los Angeles County is home to one of the nation's largest Indigenous populations: more than 160,000.

For insights on Chumash language and cultural revival efforts, see wishtoyo.org.

JOHNNY CARSON

By the time Johnny Carson delivered his final sign-off on *The Tonight Show* on May 22, 1992, the weeknight hangout in Burbank had been on the air for nearly 30 years, setting the standard for late-night. Each episode featured a monologue—maybe two dozen rapid one-liners—sketch comedy, musical performances and coveted, star-making stand-up slots. The heart of it, though, was the interview couch, where decades of notables sat in the genial glow of the host's Midwestern charisma. Before his final episode, which commanded an audience of nearly 80 million, Carson told his crew, "Everything comes to an end; nothing lasts forever. Thirty years is enough. It's time to get out while you're still working on top of your game, while you're still working well." His final remarks to the audience were given from a stool center stage: "And so it has come to this: I, uh ... am one of the lucky people in the world; I found something I always wanted to do and I have enjoyed every single minute of it. I want to thank the people who've shared this stage with me for thirty years. Mr. Ed McMahon, Mr. Doc Severinsen, and you people watching. I can only tell you that it has been an honor and a privilege to come into your homes all these years and entertain you. And I hope when I find something that I want to do and I think you would like and come back, that you'll be as gracious in inviting me into your home as you have been. I bid you a very heartfelt good night." The son of Omaha then retired to Malibu, as one might have dreamed.

RHODA RINDGE

Rhoda May Knight Rindge was either the "Queen of Malibu" or "the woman all of Southern California had grown to hate"—or both. Rhoda moved to Southern California in 1887, where she and her husband, Frederick, bought a Spanish rancho roughly half the size of Manhattan. Over the next 40 years, Rhoda, armed with a revolver strapped to her hip, fought to keep this domain private. Sometimes she won: to keep the Southern Pacific at bay, she built her own 15-mile railroad to nowhere. Sometimes she lost: today, the Pacific Coast Highway cuts through her land, despite her adamant fight against the original Roosevelt Highway. Rhoda died in 1941, but her legacy lives on. Visit her house, now a museum and California Historical Landmark, and spot the colorful tiles from her Malibu Potteries across the city.

LAGOONS

A.k.a bays, estuaries or sounds, lagoons are smaller bodies of water separated from larger ones by natural barriers, providing rich habitat for a vast array of life, from the water to the air.

BATIQUITOS LAGOON A wetland between Carlsbad and Encinitas. Site of a fine hiking trail—and, so the legend has it, long-lost pirate's treasure.

....

SEASIDE LAGOON Open throughout the summer, a man-made saltwater lagoon in Redondo Beach provides a family oasis.

....

UPPER NEWPORT BAY Due to its location on the Pacific Flyway, this estuary is a renowned stop for birders, who flock to see the over 200 species that call it home. During winter migration, as many as 35,000 birds gravitate here.

....

MALIBU LAGOON A part of Malibu Lagoon State Beach, this wetland begins where Malibu Creek runs into the Pacific Ocean. Important Chumash history here.

....

CAMPUS LAGOON This 31-acre wetland sits on the University of California, Santa Barbara campus. Listen for the chatter of the belted kingfisher while looking for blooming yerba mansa.

CHUMASH CAVE PAINTINGS

Separated from today's Santa Barbara by a 20-minute drive through historical Chumash land, Alaxuluxen, or the Chumash Painted Cave State Historic Park, offers a glimpse into the Indigenous tribe's religious connection with the land. Etched from minerals—white from limestone, black from charcoals, red from hematite or red ocher—then bound by water, plant juices, or animal fat, the paint was applied with fingers or animal-hair brushes. The site remains important to Chumash people today. Yet the paintings themselves are eroding, both from wind damage and from decades of carved initials and dates on the outside of the cave.

Learn about Chumash theories around the paintings from local elder Ernestine Ygnacio-De Soto at cyark.org/projects/chumash-painted-cave.

MOTION PICTURES

Roy Overbaugh
Director of Photography
American Film Company [*"Flying A"*], 1910-1913

I am quite sure that it will be news to most of the residents of this city that Santa Barbara was for a number of years the home and production headquarters of one of the leading motion picture companies of this country. At this early date artificial light had not been developed to the point where it was suitable for proper lighting. Consequently, all scenes were photographed by daylight. This, of course, plus certain scenic advantages, was the principle reason why the early motion picture companies chose California. It was a matter of business: they had to locate where they could depend upon the greatest number of sunny days.

Our schedule called for two completed productions each week. I should say that the pictures of that period were not the multiple-reel product of today. They were one reel only, consisting of a thousand feet. Through working together as a unit for a couple of years we had become so proficient that it took us only half a day to do a picture. If we hadn't completed it in time for a late lunch, we considered ourselves slow. This meant that we had at least four days free time each week, and then was when we all fell in love with Santa Barbara and began to appreciate the pleasures it offered. If we wanted a full week off, as we quite often did, we would work four and one half days during one week and make four pictures instead of the required two.

The company was successful and made a great deal of money, and decided that the time had come to build their own permanent studio. A site was selected on West Mission Street, extending northward and comprising the entire block between State and Chapala Streets.

"Life can be beautiful" is a familiar phrase. Well, it certainly was. Most of our time was spent at the beach.

> *One Flying A Studios building still exists in Santa Barbara: 34 W Mission St, current home of Becker Henson Niksto Architects.*

TIKI

Don the Beachcomber, Hollywood
Selected menu items, 1941

ORIGINAL RUM DRINKS

Beachcomber's Gold	$.85	Never Say Die	.85
Cobra's Fang	1.00	Nui Nui, *limit of 3*	1.40
Dr. Funk	.85	Puka Punch, *limit of 2*	1.40
Hot Rum Grog	.85	Shark's Tooth	.90
Missionary's Downfall	.85	Test Pilot, *limit of 2*	1.50
Mystery Gardenia	.85	Three Dots and a Dash	.85
Nelson's Blood	.85	Vicious Virgin	.85

ORIGINAL TROPICAL DISHES

BEACHCOMBER APPETIZERS

EGG ROLL Stuffed with minced Crab Meat, Pork, Bamboo Shoots and Water Chestnuts .90

RUMAKI Spiced Chicken Liver, Water Chestnuts wrapped in crisp Bacon .90

BARBECUED CHICKEN [*Canton Style*] Disjointed and served with Seaweed Salt 1.65

BABY SQUAB [*Canton Style*] Disjointed and served with Seaweed Salt 1.75

ENTREES

MANDARIN DUCK Boned, molded, crisped in Peanut Oil and served with Wild Plum Sauce 2.00

CHICKEN LICHEE White meat of Chicken cooked with Chinese Lichee Nuts 1.75

PORK CHOW DUN Pork, Water Chestnuts, Green Peas, sauteed and scrambled with Eggs 1.35

CHUNGKING SHRIMP Shredded Shrimps cooked with Pork, Water Chestnuts, Eggs and Green Onions 1.75

Opened in 1933 by adventurer, huckster and war hero Donn Beach [né Ernest Gantt], the Hollywood restaurant with a fabulist take on Polynesian culture and Asian cuisine is credited as the first tiki bar. The original location closed in 1985.

CHANNEL ISLANDS

This archipelago of eight islands is often called "The California Galapagos" for its notable biodiversity. Long home to the Chumash and Tongva peoples, five of the northern islands compose Channel Islands National Park.

SAN MIGUEL *Tuqan* Though the interior is riddled with ordnance from the island's days as a Navy bombing range in the 1950s, this otherwordly island contains one of the largest colonies of seals in the Pacific, tens of thousands at peak season.

SANTA ROSA *Wi'ma* Walk through a rare forest of Torrey pines on this windswept island. Hikers and paddlers revel in the opportunity to backpack to secluded beaches for camping from August to December. Rosa is also the discovery site of some of North America's most ancient human remains, 13,000+ years old.

SANTA CRUZ *Limuw* The largest of the Channel Islands, Santa Cruz is a popular first choice to visit in the national park, with large campsites, accessible kayaking tours and one of the largest sea caves in the world. It is also the setting of the Chumash creation story.

ANACAPA *Anypakh* A towering 1932 lighthouse stands on Anacapa, an island comprising three separate islets that can look like a floating pyramid on the horizon. Look for breeding rookeries of California brown pelicans and a thick border of rich kelp forests.

SANTA BARBARA *Siwot* Come spring, witness a palette of bright-yellow coreopsis flowers that take over this square-mile island, situated 38 miles from the mainland—if you can find a way to get there.

SAN NICOLAS *Haraashngna* Home to the Nicoleño Tribe of the Tongva until 1835, this remote island is now owned by the U.S. Navy, which uses it as a munitions testing site despite its endemic flora and fauna. It is well known in literature as the home of Juana Maria, who lived on the island after the Nicoleño removal, fictionalized in the popular young adult novel *Island of the Blue Dolphins*.

SANTA CATALINA *Pimu* Privately owned by descendants of William Wrigley Jr., Catalina has been turned into an island resort managed by the Catalina Island Company, with a small population of just over 4,000 residents.

SAN CLEMENTE *Kinkipar* Home to a Navy SEAL training facility. Naturalists dream of seeing the island's loggerhead shrike and song sparrow.

GEORGE FREETH

Born in Hawai'i, Freeth became one of California's first noted surfers, but also gained fame for other exploits.

"SNATCH 11 MEN FROM DEATH'S JAWS.
Heroic Venice Life Savers Rescue Fishermen Caught in Gale—
Brave Soul Plunges in Ocean Three Times to Aid Victims."

Thousands braved the gale and the flying spray, which, like heavy rain, beat inshore at Venice, yesterday afternoon, while they cheered the heroic work of the United States Volunteer Live-Saving crew as they faced the battering walls of water and rescued at their own peril the lives of eleven Japanese fishermen. George Freeth, a native of Hawaii, was the hero of the hour. Three times he plunged into a sea so wild that none dared to follow, and piloted one fishing boat through the surf; carried lifelines to another, which had upset, and helped three fishermen cling to the third craft until the life-boat could go to their rescue. The morning was clear, and from the Japanese fishing village just above the long wharf at Port Los Angeles, five boats started out early for the fishing banks. ... Shortly after noon there sprang out of the west a sudden squall. It increased in fury until the wind blew a gale and the sea rose with a rapidity which quickly drove from the big Venice pier all visitors except life-savers. ... Freeth stood with his comrades where the stinging spray drenched them, and over their heads hurtled masses of foamy waves torn on the rocky breakwater, picked up by the gale and flung half a thousand feet into the streets of the little city. Suddenly Freeth took a short run and dived into a great breaker just before it broke. The other members of the crew thought to see him dashed to death against the bulkhead. But he pierced the wall of water like a gigantic needle, and thirty feet out rose in a hollow—where the wind is calm—to take breath. Then he swam through the hearts of the waves as they thundered in, and a few moments later was in the track of the tossing skiff. ... Steering the little boat as if it was one of the surf-boards of the South Sea Isles, Freeth took it through that terrible surf, and a moment later it was beached high and dry with the aid of the daring life-savers, who rushed breast-deep into the sea to save the boat from overturning. —*Los Angeles Times*, December 17, 1908

Freeth died in 1919, killed by the Spanish influenza in San Diego. His founding role in California beach culture is commemorated by a bronze bust on Redondo Beach.

WATER

1904 Los Angeles population hits 200,000; city is running dry. Traveling by buckboard through the Newhaul-Saugus area and into the Owens Valley, William Mulholland and Fred Eaton conceive of a gravity-fed aqueduct to carry water from the valley to LA, 233 miles away.

1905 Eaton begins quietly buying Owens Valley acreage under the pretense of land reclamation and stock-raising, but is selling his land options to Los Angeles.

JUL 29, 1905 *LA Times* headline: "TITANIC PROJECT TO GIVE CITY A RIVER," detailing plans to bring water from Inyo County to the city at projected cost of $23 million. Eaton, visiting the Owens Valley with his son, is run out of town by an angry mob.

FALL 1907 A hole blasted out of solid granite marks construction of the Elizabeth Tunnel, the project's longest at more than 5 miles.

NOV 5, 1913 LA Aqueduct, made of 163 tunnels, is dedicated before 40,000 Angelenos. Mulholland declares as the sluice gates open and the water flows, "There it is. Take it!" Around 300,000,000 gallons of water go to Los Angeles daily.

1923 Farmers and ranchers form an irrigation cooperative led by Wilfred and Mark Watterson, owners of the Inyo County Bank. LA manages to secure key water rights to the co-op.

1924 High water demand in LA turns Owens Valley, once "The Switzerland of California," into a desert. The city files a lawsuit against a lengthy list of individual farmers, claiming they're diverting water that belongs to Los Angeles.

MAY 21, 1924 Dozens of Inyo County men bomb a section of the aqueduct near Lone Pine with 500 pounds of dynamite, sparking the beginning of California's "Little Civil War."

AUG 1927 The Inyo County Bank collapses, crippling valley resistance. The Watterson brothers are indicted for embezzlement, then tried and convicted on 36 counts. Lifetime savings of county residents are decimated, including payments gained from the sale of homes and ranches to Los Angeles.

1928 After another round of buyouts, Los Angeles controls 90 percent of the valley's land and water. Agriculture interests in the area are rendered obsolete.

DUKE KAHANAMOKU

The Daily Telegram, Long Beach, July 31, 1922

"DUKE KAHANAMOKU, FAMOUS SWIMMING CHAMPION, GIVES EXHIBITION ON SURF BOARD"

Duke Kahanamoku, Olympic champion and in his prime the world's greatest swimmer, gave an exhibition of surf board riding in front of the Hotel Virginia yesterday afternoon before a crowd estimated at 5000 persons. He was assisted by "Porge" Marshall, Hotel Virginia life guard, and Clarence Stark, who was stationed by the city to assist Marshall for Sunday. The local boys held their own with the Duke when it came to riding the boards even if they were not as picturesque as the Hawaiian. All of the surfers were bothered by bathers, many of whom made no effort to get out of the way. . . . It was a pretty sight to see the men come in standing up on the boards and guiding them skillfully with their feet, the surf curling away from the boards in front and at the sides. There seemed to be just one point of advantage with the Hawaiian. He kept his board at a sharp angle, giving the stunt a more picturesque appearance. But he didn't catch as many rollers as the other boys.

One of the most celebrated sportsmen of his era, Kahanamoku is widely credited with popularizing surfing on the mainland. "Duke" was his given name, not a title of nobility, though he was often referred to as "The Duke."

MARGE CALHOUN

The reporters in Honolulu were bemused. At the end of November 1958, the big world-champ surfing event was held at Mākaha Beach. Two Californians won. The *Star-Bulletin* reported: "Peter Cole, from Malibu, and Marge Calhoun from Santa Monica, were the 'culprits' who dethroned the Hawaiians." Calhoun notably stood out, a 5′ 8″ mother of two teenage girls who cheerfully described herself as living out of the trunk of a car for a month of Oahu surfing. Born in Hollywood in 1924, the "tall blonde" would go on to renown as a surf competition judge, organizer and a defining figure in California surfer style. On her passing in 2017, Calhoun was remembered as "a natural waterwoman" and "surfing's golden girl."

SURF CHAMPIONSHIPS

AN INVITATION
TO - YOU - OF
"Orange County"

SPEND THE DAY WITH US

AT THE
"Corona Del Mar Beaches"
ON EAST SIDE OF NEWPORT BAY

NEXT SUNDAY AUGUST 5TH

Pacific Coast Surf Board Championship

① Paddling race across Balboa Channel.

② Canoe tilting contest.

③ Demonstration of life saving by surf boards. [Members of the club rescued fifteen men off the Thelma when she capsized in a rough surf.]

④ Thrilling rough water surf board race from bell buoy to channel nearest east jetty.

You will see other wonderful sights during the day, such as the speed boats "whizzing" by—the airships—the sailboats—the beautiful yachts going in and out—the fishermen with their catch—the "bathers" enjoying the "still water" and "surf", the "groups" along the beaches, having—

A WONDERFUL TIME

This inaugural California surf championship was won by Tom Blake, a formative figure in West Coast surf culture. The competition continued sporadically through 1941. Blake became a nomadic author of philosophical texts, dying in 1994 at the age of 92.

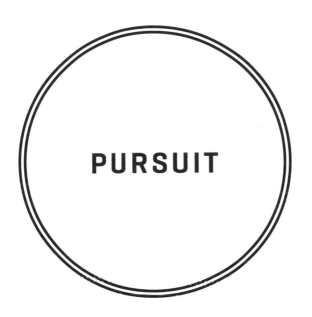

PURSUIT

A field guide to surfing on the Southern California Coast,
from history to modern etiquette, with notes on equipment,
surf spots, shops and key shapes of boards and culture

ANATOMY OF A SURFBOARD

FOIL
How volume [thickness, essentially]
is distributed across the board,
affecting performance.

NOSE
Shapes vary across board styles,
with implications for buoyancy,
paddling and maneuverablity.

STRINGER
Thin strip of wood running
nose to tail, enhancing rigidity
and riding stability.

RAILS
The edges. Thinner ["harder"]
rails reduce water resistance.
Medium is a popular choice.

ROCKER
Curve of the board's bottom,
nose to tail. Advanced surfers
tend to like more rocker.

DECK
Top of the board, where a surfer
stands. Waxing the deck is a key
part of the surfer's craft.

FINS
Standard since the 1950s.
Number [1? 3? 4?] and setup are key.

TAIL
The board's back end. Wide variety
of design, from square ["squash"] to
asymmetrical.

SURF LEXICON

CLOSEOUT The ideal wave offers an open face to surf. A closeout breaks instantly into a spitting burst of white water. A beach break is "walled up" when most waves are closeouts.

CAUGHT INSIDE Wrong time, wrong place. Results in being tossed by the white water from breaking waves. Steady paddling, duck-diving under each approaching wave is the only way out.

DUCK DIVE Essential trick. As a wave approaches, surfers shove boards underwater. Diving under the wave, they surface on the other side.

GOOFY AND REGULAR Surfer's stances. Regulars stand with right foot on the board's tail. Goofy footers stand left foot back.

GLASSY Surfers dream of a mirror-smooth ocean, no wind. In Southern California, it's often glassy early, before onshore winds arrive. Wind-swept waves are "textured" or "blown out."

LEFT AND RIGHT Waves have direction. On a left, the open face of the wave is to the surfer's left; on a right, the opposite. Some breaks, like Trestles, have a left *and* a right.

LINEUP The group of surfers at a spot. Might be crowded or, hopefully, empty. Wide variety of skill levels makes for a "hectic" lineup.

OUTSIDE The area beyond the breaking waves. Sometimes, a bigger peak will pop up farther out, and a surfer in the lineup will say, "Outside!" Paddle hard for the horizon.

PITTED Riding deep enough in a barreling wave to disappear from view. Popularized by viral interview with Micah Peasley at The Wedge in Newport Beach. Often used ironically.

RIP CURRENT Current running from beach out to sea. Sand-bottomed breaks often result in murky churn, with fewer breaking waves in the rip zone. A strong rip can be dangerous, but some surfers use them as a high-speed train to the lineup.

SET Waves move in sets. How many waves depends on the swell characteristics. It could be a 10-wave set or a two-wave set.

SWELL A series of regular waves, born from winds of a low-pressure system out at sea. *Wind swell* refers to waves created by near-shore winds. Typically, the waves from groundswells, formed by offshore storms, are cleaner, more powerful.

SURFING ESSENTIALS

SURFBOARDS

For beginners, the best choice is a soft-top, or "foamie," without a hard fiberglass deck. Soft-tops vary in size, but an 8-foot board is a good place to start. From there, surfboards become a matter of personal style. Shorter boards turn more quickly, feeling more maneuverable. A classic longboard imparts a smooth, gliding feeling.

WET SUITS

Southern California water temps run cool. Many surfers wear full suits even in summer. For winter sessions in Ventura and Santa Barbara, you may want a hooded suit, booties and gloves.

LEASHES

Pat O'Neill is credited with inventing the surf leash in 1971. Until then, loose boards littered the lineup, smashed into cliffs [and heads] and sent surfers in frantic chase. A retro-inspired movement has turned against leashes of late. But in a crowded lineup, they're a good idea.

TIDES

Due to its proximity, the moon is the most powerful among the forces that control the tides, and the widest swings coincide with the new and full moon phases. California has two high and two low tides each lunar day. Most surf spots work well around 3 feet.

ETIQUETTE

Surf etiquette can appear arcane. Approach the lineup with a friendly attitude, and you're off to a good start. At the take-off point, the surfer closest to where the wave is breaking has right of way. He is sitting deepest, and it's his wave. Paddling around the back of him to get into a deeper position—backpaddling—is never cool. If a surfer is riding a wave, do not paddle and try to take off in front of her. When paddling back out to the peak from the inside, always be aware of your surroundings. Be courteous to the surfers riding waves. When the lineup is comparatively uncrowded, allow other surfers to get their fair share of waves. Don't immediately paddle to the front of the line when you reach the peak. And if your friend calls "party wave," paddle and go!

SEASONS

Waves shift with the seasons; surfers follow them. Winter swells originate from low-pressure systems that spin up in the North Pacific; typically winter surf offers more-powerful swells. Sometimes the low passes very close to the coast, generating north winds as it does. Brave the biting cold in Ventura to experience some of the best waves of the year.

Beginning in the spring, the South Pacific awakens and sends swells from more distant storms. Malibu turns on. Beach breaks like Huntington Beach shift to more lefts, as the waves arrive from the south. Later in the summer, hurricanes manifest in Baja and deliver an extra punch to the surf in Southern California. In August 2014, Hurricane Marie lit up the coast with uniquely large swells.

Fall is a magic time at the beach breaks. Combo swells converge from both the north and south to create perfect A-frame peaks. The Santa Ana winds blow offshore and send spray flying out to sea. Held back by the wind, waves break more slowly, offering more space to turn or slide into the barrel. For a session to remember, surf at sunset as the warm Santa Anas blow.

FORECASTS

Checking surf forecasts regularly can yield surprise rewards. Groundswells form well out to sea, easiest to predict. Satellites measure wind speeds and track low pressure as it forms. Forecasters estimate a wave's size and arrival. Local weather plays a role. Rogue winds can destroy even the most perfect groundswell. Wind swell—more difficult to predict—forms spontaneously from near-shore weather patterns.

> *Surf information has become readily accessible in this digital age. Surfline, Magicseaweed and Windfinder are among the go-to sources for live updates on wave conditions.*

SURF FILMS OF NOTE

GIDGET 1959 Sandra Dee plays the exuberant teen Gidget: "Surfing is out of this world!" More than any other, this film injected surfing into the mainstream and brought crowds flocking to the beach to try it out.

....

THE ENDLESS SUMMER 1965 Bruce Brown tracks Mike Hynson and Robert August around the world. Deadpan narration, big-name cameos remain much-imitated. Brown's *On Any Sunday* is a motorcycle classic.

....

BIG WEDNESDAY 1978 "No one knows where the waves come from." A group of friends surf, pull pranks and come of age in the shadow of the Vietnam War.

....

POINT BREAK 1991 Kathryn Bigelow's beachside heist film recruited real-life pro surfers to play secondary bad guys and stand in for Keanu Reeves and Patrick Swayze when the waves got intense. A cult favorite, source of many lines quoted in and out of context.

....

ONE CALIFORNIA DAY 2007 Narrated by respected surfer Devon Howard, this documentary travels the coast. Appearances by legends such as Tom Curren, Greg Noll and Skip Frye. Filmed in Super 16mm.

BOARD SHAPERS

A snapshot of Southern California's vibrant board-building community.

FURROW SURF CRAFT Growing up, Christine Caro doodled fish-shaped boards in school notebooks and haunted a local vintage-board shop. These days, label Furrow reinterprets late-'60s designs. *furrowsurfcraft.com*

BING SURFBOARDS Storied label, best known for longboards. In the 1960s, Bing Copeland opened a shop and glass factory in Hermosa Beach. Today, Matt Calvani, who learned shaping from masters like Wayne Lynch and Hap Jacobs, runs the Encinitas factory. *bingsurf.com*

CHRISTENSON SURFBOARDS Everything from performance shortboards and big-wave guns to unique custom boards. Learned from legends Art Brewer and Skip Frye. *christensonsurfboards.com*

...LOST SURFBOARDS Matt Biolos started as a sander at Catalyst in San Clemente and has built Lost into a global brand, sponsoring top pros. Specializes in performance shortboards. *lostsurfboards.net*

ALBUM SURF Matt Parker made his first board in his garage in 2001. His fine-art background fosters innovation: Album is known for unique shapes, eye-catching colors and finishes. *albumsurf.com*

STAMPS SURFBOARDS Seal Beach native Tim Stamps says resin, foam dust, and salt water run through his veins. Stamps has made performance shortboards for top professionals Brett Simpson and Courtney Conlogue. Mid-lengths, fish, logs, shortboards. *surfboardsbystamps.com*

DAVENPORT SURFBOARDS Growing up in Redondo Beach, Adam Davenport would pass storied workshops [Hap Jacobs, Greg Noll] on his walk to the pier. He now handcrafts vintage-inspired longboards in Ventura. *davenportsurfboards.com*

CHANNEL ISLANDS SURFBOARDS Founded in 1969 by Al Merrick, best known for high-performance shortboards. HQ sits not far from Rincon, the perfect test track. *cissurfboards.com*

RYAN LOVELACE SURFCRAFT Santa Barbara shaper with a rep for handcrafted boards. Made-to-order mid-lengths, like the twin-fin FM and the v.Bowls, are especially coveted. Stock boards under the Love Machine label. *rlovelace.com*

SURF SHOPS

SOUTH COAST SURF SHOP Started in 1974, with locations in Ocean Beach and Pacific Beach. Wide selection of boards, wetsuits and clothing. *5023 Newport Ave, Ocean Beach and 740 Felspar St, Pacific Beach*

MITCH'S SURF SHOP Since 1967. Boards from Takayama, Christenson, Tomo, Mandala, Gary Hanel and Rainbow. Diving gear rentals. *631 Pearl St, La Jolla and 363 N Hwy101, Solana Beach*

HANSEN SURFBOARDS Family owned since 1961, a block from storied surf spot Swami's. Boards from Firewire, Lost, Channel Islands and more. Rentals. *1105 S Coast Hwy 101, Encinitas*

REAL SURF SHOP Family-owned wood-sided yellow cottage housing a shop and the shaping room for Shawn Ambrose boards. *1101 S Coast Hwy, Oceanside*

HOBIE SURF SHOP Just two blocks from where Hobie Alter opened So-Cal's first balsa-board-shaping shop. *34174 Pacific Coast Hwy, Dana Point*

THALIA SURF SHOP Boards from Tyler Warren, Alex Knost, Greg Liddle and more. Used boards, lessons, rentals, frequent events and film nights. *915 S Coast Hwy, Laguna Beach*

ALMOND SURF SHOP Home to the brand's playfully elegant boards and a source of how-to info and smart surf-culture mementos. *1720 Santa Ana Ave, Costa Mesa*

BROTHERS MARSHALL SURF SHOP AND CULTURAL CENTER Malibu fixtures Trace and Chad Marshall are known for creativity. A surf shop, art gallery and events space. *21237 Pacific Coast Hwy, Malibu*

TRAVELER SURF CLUB Locker rooms, hot showers and beach cruisers. *22941 Pacific Coast Hwy, Malibu and 228 E Thompson Blvd, Ventura*

VENTURA SURF SHOP Long-standing locally owned shop, around the corner from C Street surf spot. *88 E Thompson, Ventura*

SURF N' WEAR BEACH HOUSE Founded in 1962. Beach supplies and clothing up front, boards and wet suits in the back. Vintage boards hang from the roof. Longtime home to shaper Renny Yater. *10 State St, Santa Barbara*

MOLLUSK SURF SHOP Curated boards and beach-culture aesthetics. *208 Gray Ave, Santa Barbara and 1600 Pacific Ave, Venice Beach*

SURF SCHOOLS

Select places to learn the waves.

SAN DIEGO SURF SCHOOL
Private and group lessons. More than 20 years' experience. *Pacific Beach, sandiegosurfingschool.com*

EBONY BEACH CLUB
Paddle-outs, lessons, special events, second Sunday of each summer month. *Manhattan Beach, ebonybeachclub.com*

SURF HAPPENS
Owned by former pro surfer Chris Keet. Lessons and weekly camps for all ages and abilities. *Santa Barbara, surfhappens.com*

GIRL IN THE CURL
Youth classes [5 and up] emphasized, but all ages served. *Doheny State Beach, Dana Point, girlinthecurl.com*

MALIBU MAKOS
Private and group lessons since 1991. *Zuma Beach, malibumakos.com*

OHANA SURF CAMP
Private and group lessons at Mondos, a beginner-friendly break. *Ventura, ohanasurfcamp.com*

SURF DIVA
Twins Izzy and Coco Tihanyi started Surf Diva as a school for women. It has since expanded, and offers lessons for surf and SUP for all ages and abilities. *La Jolla Shores, surfdiva.com*

ENDLESS SUN SURF SCHOOL
Individual, private group lessons since 1963. Women-only groups available too. *Newport Beach Pier, endlesssunsurf.com*

WAVEHUGGERS
Private and group lessons with an environmental consciousness: cleanups, wet-suit upcycling, partnerships. *San Diego, Orange County, LA, wavehuggers.com*

HB SURF SCHOOL
Lessons for all ages and abilities since 2007. Licensed by the City of Huntington Beach. *Huntington Beach Pier, hbsurfschool.com*

SURFIN FIRE
Owner Jon "JP" Peterson is a 36-year veteran of the Encinitas Fire Department. *Encinitas, Carlsbad, Oceanside, surfinfire.com*

For a course in surf history, see The Encyclopedia of Surfing. *eos.surf*

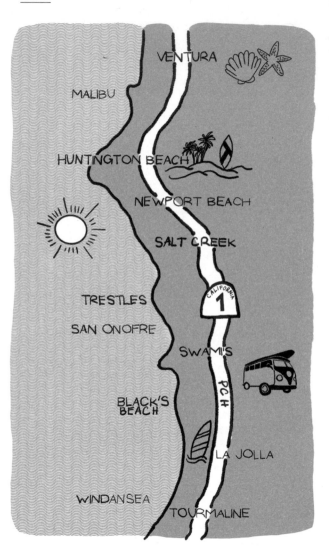

SURF SPOTS

Select places to learn the waves, north to south.

C STREET *Ventura* Sprawling right point. Something for everyone. Rip the upper section ["Pipe"] on a shortboard; lower section California Street is an easy-riding beginner zone.

MALIBU SURFRIDER BEACH *Malibu* Southern California's diva: a picturesque right point break. Cher's house sits on the bluff above the beach. The wave: a dreamy green wall.

HUNTINGTON BEACH *Orange County* Find the best waves near the pier, or cruise the beach for a less-crowded peak. Hit it early to avoid afternoon onshore wind.

NEWPORT BEACH *Orange County* Jetties run between Newport Beach pier and the Santa Ana river. Especially good in the fall when Santa Anas blow; 54th and 56th streets stand out.

SALT CREEK *Dana Point* Variety, depending on swell and season. Cruise the Point's mellow left. Bring a shortboard for punchy peaks at Middles.

TRESTLES *San Clemente* Breaking over a cobble-rock bottom, the perfect A-frame wave. The lineup is stacked with local and regional pros.

SAN ONOFRE *San Clemente* Some of SoCal's best longboard waves. Keep it easy at Old Man's or show style at The Point and Church.

SWAMI'S *Encinitas* Named for a nearby spiritual center. Steep peak outside, mellow right through the inside. The parking lot is a vibe.

BLACK'S *Torrey Pines State Beach* Sand-bottom beach break. Powerful left when winter swells collide with underwater canyon.

LA JOLLA SHORES *La Jolla* An easy, sand-bottom beach break: perfect spot to learn. Bring a longboard or rent a soft-top.

WINDANSEA *La Jolla* Local classic breaks left and right over a shallow reef. A landmark thatched-roof shack stands on the cliffs.

TOURMALINE SURFING PARK *San Diego* Dedicated in 1965, the first beach park in the U.S. specifically for surfing. Bring a longboard.

RINCON *San Diego County* The Queen of the Coast, among the world's best right point breaks. Small days perfect for bigger boards. Winter swell creates an expert's playground.

PERSPECTIVES

"Our surf experience is shaped by the time of our initiation. For me, that was the mid-to-late '70s. At its best, California surfing represented a non-try-hard attitude. There was still a connection to Hawaiian and Mainland roots—a hangover from the early Californian micro-diaspora to Oahu in the early '50s. It had precisely zero to do with contests, and everything to do with travel, experience, dirtbagging and not caring about the squares. Running down a chattering blue wall, laughing audibly, with no one except maybe a dipping tern to witness. Madness. So good."

— SCOTT HULET, former owner of The Longboard Grotto Surf Shop and creative director at *The Surfer's Journal*

"Living inland, we were weekend warriors. On Saturday, we called the phone numbers to get the surf report because we didn't have live webcams then. My dad would go, 'So where do you think is good today?' I always wanted to go to Lowers. We would spend all day at Lowers, from sunup to sundown. No matter what the conditions were, it was a good day, because I was doing what I loved. And at the end of the day, my brother and sister and I would race each other up the hill."

—COURTNEY CONLOGUE, World Championship Tour surfer, two-time US Open winner

"I feel like the different types of boards are like different genres of music. Learning to play them all, you need to know what you're getting into from the start. The way I ride a longboard is different from the way I ride one of my asymmetric shortboards. But it's all connected, because it's all surfing. You're still out there trying to time a wave and trying to predict what's going to happen. I can take anything I want that floats out into the ocean and, you know, express myself on it."

—RYAN BURCH, pro surfer and shaper

"Surfing is an odd disease. It takes over a life as a principal motivating factor, but what is it, exactly? Exercise? Meditation? A little bit of me time? It demands primary attention though it is the most pointless, utterly pointless, thing a person can do in any given moment. But there it is, demanding. Maybe it's why surfing survives. Its pointlessness transcends real life and, thus, shifts the meaning of 'real' altogether. Surfers exist in a dream state surrounded by like-minded dreamers. Or idiots. Take your pick."

—CHAS SMITH, author of *Welcome to Paradise, Now Go to Hell* and producer of *Trouble: The Lisa Andersen Story*

INTERVIEWS

Ten conversations with locals of note about writing, weather,
surfing, culinary heritage, coastal wetlands, beach access,
the joy of rollerskating and more

CARLOS SALGADO

CHEF

I'M THROUGH-AND-THROUGH Orange County. I moved here before I even remember anything.

MY PARENTS HAD what you would call a hole-in-the-wall Mexican restaurant, serving your typical generalized Mexican food: crispy shredded beef, shredded chicken tacos with jack cheese, lettuce and the tomato wedge.

I GREW UP at the family table in the dining room, the closest one to the back, to the cash register. We would do our homework, watch some cartoons in the back office.

HELPING TO WASH dishes, fill fountain drinks, pack to-go orders. It wasn't optional.

MY DAD'S FAMILY is from Guerrero. My mom is from Jalisco, near Guadalajara, so we grew up with a lot of what we call "the guisado."

THE SLOW-COOKING CUTS. Often the cheaper ones, right? Dark meat, leg meat or off-cuts.

THEN, MOM AND DAD'S hybrid cuisine: getting salt-and-pepper fish from the Chinese restaurant and eating that with tortillas and Mom's homemade salsa. Like a makeshift fish taco.

WHEN I STARTED planning Taco María, my grandmother was still alive. I remember listening intently as she told me the *passes*—the raisins—or the *ciruelas*—the dried plums—that she would use.

THAT'S THE flavor profile I based every mole I've ever made on.

VIRTUALLY EVERY WOMAN in my family is named María.

DESPITE BEING a sit-down, Michelin-star restaurant, we make it a point to do seasonal tamales by the dozen or half dozen. A cultural touchstone.

IN SOUTHERN CALIFORNIA right now, you can easily find some of the best tortillas in the world. We're proud to say we're one of those.

MAKĀLA HARMONY SMITH

SURFER

I WAS BORN and raised in Dana Point. Laguna Beach is just 20 minutes north.

THE FIRST RECORD of my family coming to Southern California was specifically for the Festival of the Arts in Laguna Beach, which has been going since the '20s or even before. They traveled from Europe with a box of ceramics.

FISHERMEN. Artists coming to the ocean for inspiration. Florists who traveled for the agriculture around here.

ARTISTS AND SURFERS. That community basically inspired what I've blossomed into as a person.

IN THE '40S all the way to the '60s, Dana Point was such a mecca. One of the best waves in California. People don't know that now, because of the harbor that was built in the '60s.

I WOULD SURF before I could even swim, on the front of my dad's board. I got my own board when I was five or six.

I RIDE A longboard. Everything I ride is a very traditional, 1960s-vintage-type thing.

HOBIE SURFBOARDS IS right up the street from me. As a kid growing up, that was always the team to be part of.

I DESIGNED THREE different models with Hobie: a longboard, a mid-length and a short board. I worked directly with the shaper.

WHAT IS IT you want to do with this craft? I love going fast. I really like point-break-style waves. So a 50-50 rail angle is what I look for.

BUT IT'S ALSO the fabric and colors, how it will look in the shop, everything.

SURFING HAS JUST boomed. The number of people in the water is bananas. But the community itself, it's like the heart just grows fonder. It stays the same.

WENDY KATAGI

WATERSHED PLANNER, SONGWRITER

I'VE BEEN WRITING songs recently about nature.

"STEELHEAD RUN" IS about how it's time to make the change, bring down barriers, both literally—fish passage barriers—and figuratively, in our mindset.

IT WAS INSPIRED by over a decade of work—not just in Orange County but multiple watersheds in Southern California.

IT'S MIMICKING THE movement of fish as they migrate upstream, then back to the ocean.

STEELHEAD START OFF as rainbow trout. When they go to the ocean, they transform.

THEY ARE SO big, like 2 to 3 feet, dwarfing any kind of fish in the river. They move like ships.

THERE ARE soft-bottom areas of the LA River that are beautiful. Teeming with wildlife.

AND THEN THERE are other areas that are concrete-lined.

EVERYBODY KIND OF turned their back on this river.

A COMPLETELY polluted river system, with so little water that all you see is algae growing?

THAT IS NOT a sustainable future for Angelenos, or anybody really, right?

WE'RE ADDING A deeper channel in opportunistic areas to create the velocities and depths that will support the steelhead migration.

THERE'S SOME AREAS where we can bring back the floodplain and do some huge restoration.

WE NEED TO co-exist with these amazing species. The steelhead, the mountain lion: these iconic species.

IF YOU BRING them back, you bring back a whole host of native species.

THAT MEANS YOU'RE doing something right.

DAVE ALLEE

FOUNDER, ALMOND SURFBOARDS

I WAS BORN and raised in Costa Mesa, grew up two blocks away from where the Almond shop now sits on Santa Ana Avenue.

ME AND MY friends, we were just on bikes all summer long.

YOU THROW FINS and a towel in your bike basket and you're straight down the hill.

BUT ANYONE who thinks surfing is a summer sport is missing out on the sweetest time to be in the water.

IN JANUARY, WE get these high-pressure, windless days, beautiful surfing conditions. A far-off winter storm will bring groundswells from the northwest.

AT SAN ONOFRE, there's Trestles, Churches, Four Doors, Old Man's, Dogpatch. Every break has a different name.

FOUR DOORS IS named for a utility building nearby that has four doors. Shocker. Surfers are incredibly clever.

WHEN I THINK of who the Almond customer is, I often think about surfers who are not too different from myself. And I'd describe myself as the "eager intermediate."

I UNDERSTAND the average, everyday surfer. I'm not an ex-pro. I'm the 36-year-old guy with two kids who, if I can sneak in a 45-minute session once a week, I am stoked. But I have been thinking about surfing and surfboards for a long time.

FRIDAY MORNINGS at 32nd Street in Newport. I secretly call the spot "Magic Johnson's."

THERE'S THE EARLY morning crowd that's in the water at 7:00. Out by 8:50 so they can make it to work on time. Gentleman's Hour starts when that crew leaves. Thin crowds, plenty of waves in the morning.

I DON'T KNOW their names, but there are guys I've surfed with for years. There's a camaraderie of sitting 6 feet apart out there, giving the knowing nod: "That was a good one."

....

WHEN I WAS shaping my first surfboard, I got to go spend four or five hours with Terry Martin. He has since passed, but he was the head shaper at Hobie for decades. I believe he hand-shaped something like 100,000 boards in his career.

....

I WAS 19 years old. What I remember, more than any technical advice he gave, was just how open-handed he was with his knowledge. He made me feel important.

....

AT ALMOND, we try to be the same way. There are no stupid questions. I remember being the kooky kid coming into a surf shop.

....

THE CALIFORNIA SHAPERS who laid the foundations started in the early 1950s with balsa wood surfboards.

....

UP AND DOWN the PCH—San Diego, Solana, Dana Point, Newport—all these places had their local shaper's shop. Storefronts with boards in the windows and the guy's name on a sign.

....

WE CAN TRACE Almond's lineage to the early guys. Our head

shaper, Griffin, learned from Bruce Jones, who learned from Phil Edwards, who shaped at Hobie.

....

I WANT an Almond board to work in 50 years. I want them to look good in 50 years.

....

THE NAME? It's a food. It's a shape. It's a color. It's California. And I like the shape of the word.

....

A FLATTER ROCKER, a little kick in the tail, enough shape in the nose so you don't pearl and nosedive.

....

THE DAYS WHERE I'm trying to stand up with a wave that's already breaking on top of me are the days where I'm like, "Did I forget how to do any of this?"

....

BUT IF YOU can scratch the wave two strokes earlier, everything else falls into place.

....

WHEN I WAS just starting, my friend's dad lent me his old 1964 Hobie. It was like having this amazing old car.

....

YOU CAN LAY it out on a piece of Masonite, trace it and use that curve. You combine it and blend it and widen it.

....

YOU USE THAT as a starting point for something new.

TINA SEGURA

COAST ADVOCATE

I GOT INTO Pepperdine law school. If you go to school near a perfect surf break, you take advantage of that.

WHILE YOU'RE waiting for Bar results, it's a couple months of in-between time. You're not getting hired. I decided to volunteer with Surfrider.

I HAD INTERNED at the public defender's office throughout law school. But, on the other hand, I was getting more involved with ocean advocacy.

I'M AN ENFORCEMENT officer for the California Coastal Commission, using my law degree to protect the coast, from Topanga up to San Luis Obispo County.

IF SOMEONE reports signs that say "PRIVATE BEACH"— what's the deal? I go inspect. If someone says, "Hey, habitat got bulldozed," we check.

GENERALLY, the beach below the high-tide line is public. It's a difficult thing to ascertain. Wet sand is a good marker. Or, when you're walking along the beach and see kelp washed up on the shore, that's usually a good indicator.

ONE THING NEAR and dear to my heart is equitable access. Who's lucky enough to live at the coast? Who's excluded?

I'M THE DAUGHTER of an immigrant; my family's Mexican American. First-generation college graduate. First-generation law school graduate, for sure.

WHEN I WAS learning to surf, Old Man's in San Clemente was the first beach where someone actually cheered me into a wave.

I STARTED LEARNING in Malibu, and had a few older, white, experienced surfers yell at me. Just scary vibes in the water.

SO OLD MAN'S is a special place for me. The waves are long and mellow. It feels like you traveled back in time to the '70s. People with vans. Families grilling and hanging out.

DANA OLSEN

FARMER

JOHN GIVENS FARM is just me and John. That's it.

SANTA BARBARA HAS this incredible climate. A great number of days in the 70s: ideal for vegetable growing.

IN THE LATE '40s and '50s, Goleta was the United States' lemon-growing capital, before the citrus production moved to Florida.

THIS LAND ON Ward Drive was an abandoned lemon orchard. They pulled a bunch of stumps and leveled the land.

JOHN USED TO call it a "shotgun approach": a little of everything. Greens, chards, kales, lettuces. We grow weirdo greens like endive, escarole, frisee.

KOHLRABI, artichokes, arugula, asparagus, beans, beets, cabbages. We're big carrot growers.

CUCUMBERS and zucchini. Heirloom tomatoes, slicer tomatoes, cherry tomatoes and romas. We've got eggplant and strawberries.

JOHN WAS ONE of the first people ever at the Santa Barbara Farmers Market. In the mid-'80s, the organic movement was starting to take off.

THERE ARE FARMERS who aren't certified organic, but they don't spray much.

IT'S GREAT TO be certified. But it's better if you're a good farmer.

NOW I'M sales manager, and I play guitar for Area 51, a local dance band.

A LOT OF my friends say, "Man, you must have a really idyllic lifestyle. You play music and you work on an organic farm." I say, "Hey, I play the same crummy clubs you play!"

FARMING IS HARD work. Not a lot of romance in it.

BUT IT'S NICE to be able to work for yourself and see the …

… NOT TO be punny, but the fruits of your labor and all.

SHELLEY KLEYN ARMISTEAD

HOSPITALITY CEO

WE MAKE OVER 150 products at Gjusta. Cans, bottles, jars. Bread and pastries. There's dine-in, catering, a massive wholesale operation, events. Our staff at Gjusta alone is 183 people.

....

THAT'S 183 OPPORTUNITIES for conversation. Learning how to navigate people, their interests and communication.

....

WE MOVED TO Venice in 2008.

....

I WAS PREGNANT with my second son. I felt instantly drawn to Venice because of its proximity to the ocean.

....

IT WAS LESS put-together than Santa Monica. Friendly.

....

GJELINA HAD BEEN open for five months, and I'd go with my kids on Sundays for breakfast. And of course, Gjelina was painfully cool, and they put everyone with kids in a room off to the side.

....

THE PERSON I sat next to the most frequently was the founder, Fran Camaj. His mother is Gjelina.

I STARTED AS chief operating officer in 2014. My first project was opening Gjusta.

....

THE CHAOS DRIVES us. You're constantly ducking, moving, in conversation. Anybody who's in hospitality has the neurological process that needs the noise in order to stay focused.

....

OVER 70 PERCENT of our staff is from Oaxaca. Without their creativity, we lock the doors.

....

IMMIGRANT COMMUNITIES have an enormous amount of pressure that we could never understand.

....

I STARTED GOING down to Oaxaca. I'd take photographs with me and meet their families.

....

THE MARBLE ON the bar at Gjusta is reclaimed from decades ago. It's three and a half inches thick. The counters are all old oak.

....

THOSE DETAILS CREATE a sense of place. A massive stability, without you knowing it.

MADDALENA BEARZI

MARINE BIOLOGIST, NONPROFIT DIRECTOR

YOU CAN SEE dolphins from the coastline in Los Angeles—that's what I always tell people.

THE COAST OF Southern California has an amazing diversity of marine mammals.

BOTTLENOSE dolphins, common dolphins, Pacific white-sided dolphins, blue whales, gray whales, minke whales, humpback whales, fin whales, orcas and many more.

YOU CAN SEE pinnipeds, like California sea lions, harbor seals, elephant seals.

I WAS BORN in Verona, Italy.

WHEN I MOVED to LA, I was sailing with my husband—he's a Hollywood native—and I started seeing all these dolphins and whales.

I DISCOVERED that nobody had ever studied these animals here.

MY HUSBAND AND I co-founded Ocean Conservation Society.

WHAT AT THE BEGINNING was mostly research, over time became more conservation.

WE ARE IN such a dire situation right now that we don't have the luxury to do just research.

I'M A BEHAVIORAL ecologist; I love to study the behavior of these animals.

BUT I DON'T feel like just studying the behavior without taking the responsibility. To protect them is the right thing to do.

THE FIRST TIME I encountered a blue whale, I was out on rough water near Catalina Island on a 20-foot little powerboat.

SUDDENLY THIS WHALE just emerged next to the boat.

THE BLOW HOLE was as big as the cabin on my boat, and I really felt like a toothpick.

THE BEAUTY, THE power and the grace of these animals in the water is amazing to witness.

TERRANCE BROWN

SKATE CLUB FOUNDER

SKATING BRINGS people out of their shells. I get bubbly, I get these butterflies.

WHEN YOU PUT on these skates, man, it just gets you so high up. It's such a magical feeling. It's like, *I am unstoppable.*

SB ROLLERS STARTED at the beginning of COVID.

I WAS WORKING as a trainer with professional athletes, and like most people, business was not doing well for me.

MY MOM MENTIONED skating; she was trying to get my spirit up. I never skated in my life, but I was intrigued. I found an instructor, Sonny, the owner of Skating Plus in Ventura.

THE REST OF the class, I think the ages were seven to 10.

BUT THE KIDS made me feel so comfortable. They were, like, coaching me through it.

I'D GO ON the bike path, and I would see maybe one or two skaters. I'd tell them, "Let's link up, start this little meetup and we can do routines.

IT'S LIKE DANCING on skates."

AS WE SKATED, we would see other skaters and pull them in. From there, it just grew.

WE'LL START SYNCHING the same moves, and people will walk by and start watching.

IT'S LIKE WE'RE putting on the show for Santa Barbara, for all the tourists and all the locals.

WE HAVE A MEETUP every Sunday. We have live DJs; we play funk, soul music, rap, techno.

EVERYONE IS WELCOME.

THE ONLY THING I'm mad about is that I didn't do this a long time ago.

I STILL GET depressed at times, but soon as it hits, I know where to go.

STORIES

Essays and selected writing by noted
voices from the Southern California Coast

COASTLINE OF THE MIND

Written by **STEVE POND**

ABOUT 25 YEARS AGO, on assignment for the 20th-anniversary issue of *Rolling Stone* magazine, I stood on the balcony of Brian Wilson's house in Malibu, a modest structure with a spectacular view of the Pacific from a cliff that overlooked a small stretch of beach. The swells were nothing special that afternoon. But that hadn't deterred the dozen or so surfers on the waves below us. So I had to ask the man who'd written "Surfer Girl," "Surfin' U.S.A.," "Surf City," and "The Lonely Surfer" if he ever looked out from his balcony and thought about how his influence might draw people to these Southern California beaches to surf. Wilson, never a big-picture kind of guy, demurred. "No, I don't," he said. "I think about Phil Spector's influence."

Maybe it makes sense. Wilson, after all, was never a surfer himself, and only started writing those surf songs because his brother Dennis, the one true beach boy in The Beach Boys, told him, "Hey, surfing's getting really big. You guys ought to write a song about it." And while the songs he wrote initially seemed simple and sunny, he paid the price for the fame they brought him: The pressures got to his already fragile mental state, and drugs exacerbated his fears until he broke down and withdrew from the band and the world. When we met, Wilson was nervous, jittery and reluctant to address the reverberations of his songs, though was also clearly aware of the impact the music and the image had: About 15 minutes after saying he never thought about his influence on the surfers, Wilson suddenly sat up and pulled off his T-shirt. "There," he said. "Now I look like a *real* Beach Boy."

How did he know what a real Beach Boy was supposed to look like? Through movies, through music [including his own], through the whole hedonistic myth whipped up by assorted Gidgets and Surfaris and canny businessmen who, while trying to catch the wave of a fad, found themselves creating a Southern California coastline of the mind that both captivates and haunts the culture to this day.

In a few short years—1961 through 1964, really, though it felt longer than that—surf music and surf movies created the image of Southern California that still persists. It was escapism, it was purposeful teen mythologizing, and damned if it didn't work—to lure people to SoCal, to give the ones who didn't come something to imagine, and to give those who did a bubble to puncture.

Hell, the Eagles' "Hotel California" [*You can check out any time you like/But you can never leave*] and Randy Newman's "I Love L.A." [*Look at that mountain, look at those trees/Look at that bum over there, he's down on his knees*] lose their ability to mock if you don't at least partially buy the ideal. As Newman sang, both with his tongue in his cheek and his heart on his sleeve, *Roll down the window, put down the top/Crank up the Beach Boys, baby/Don't let the music stop.*

That all of this was designed to capitalize on a fad is amusing in retrospect; surf music and surf movies died out pretty quickly in one way, but they never really died in a way that matters. And surfing itself wasn't a fad at all; it's still around, still the same sport it always was. Surfers were out there in 1957, complaining about *Gidget* and *Beach Blanket Bingo*; they're out there now, and as a group they don't really care what pop culture says about them. As Guy Trebay wrote in *The New York Times* in 2006, "It is possible that no sport practiced by fewer people has ever had the influence of surfing on American style."

But it took some help to have that influence. While surfing had been taking place in California since the early 20th century, after being imported from Hawai'i, by the middle of the century, it was a niche sport. Its practitioners were typically laid-back, eccentric and far from the straitlaced mainstream. In that last sense, they shared something with nascent rock 'n' rollers and surly, charismatic icons like Marlon Brando and James Dean and the early Elvis—as much threats as entertainers in some eyes.

In the mid-1950s, a screenwriter named Frederick Kohner, living in tony Brentwood, heard the stories his teenage daughter told about the surfers she met on the beach at Malibu. Kohner's daughter Kathy had been nicknamed "Gidget"—i.e., "girl midget," for her short stature—by one of the guys on the beach, and in short order, her stories became a novel, *Gidget, the Little Girl with Big Ideas*, which became a Columbia Pictures comedy shot in 26 days, launching the beach-party genre.

Kohner was an immigrant from Austria-Hungary; director Paul Wendkos was a Philadelphia native and World War II vet who started out in documentaries; and star Sandra Dee a Jersey girl on the path to be a serious actress after *Until They Sail* and *Imitation of Life*. Yet this unlikely creative team and *Gidget* dragged surf culture—or its version, which of course most real surfers disdained—into the mainstream. More than that, it put a new spin on the teen comedies and rock-'n'-roll-spiked dramas of the '50s, and gave them somewhere new to go: the beach.

By the early '60s, legendary producer Samuel Arkoff, who never met a fad he couldn't exploit in quite entertaining fashion, set his American International Pictures to making a string of films that pretty much defined the genre, almost all of them featuring Frankie Avalon and Annette Funicello. *Beach Party* was the first. *Beach Blanket Bingo* held the crown for the best title for all of three months in 1965, before it was usurped by *How to Stuff a Wild Bikini* and then, four months after that, *Dr. Goldfoot and the Bikini Machine*. Elvis himself mounted a board in *Blue Hawaii*.

Meanwhile, practitioners in Elvis' old stomping grounds, rock 'n' roll, took notice of surfing as well. Even before Brian Wilson's brother urged him to write about the surfing boom, a Boston-born guitarist was selling out his house-band gig at the Rendezvous Ballroom in Balboa, right by Newport Beach in Orange County. Dick Dale and His Del-Tones worked in the tradition of guitar-based instrumental rock that began in the '50s with the likes of Duane Eddy and Link Wray. But Dale pushed it in a distinctive direction, beginning with "Let's Go Trippin'" in 1961. Armed with a Fender Stratocaster guitar, a Fender reverb unit and a Dual Showman amplifier, he created a driving sound, dripping with reverb, that became known as surf music.

Did it sound like surfing? What does surfing sound like? Dale was a surfer, and he said he designed his sound to capture the feeling of catching a wave. Who could argue when he took an old song of Eastern Mediterranean origin, "Misirlou," and revved it up into one of the greatest rock instrumentals anybody had heard? If Dick said it was surf music, it was surf music. And so was "Pipeline" by The Chantays and "Wipe Out" by The Surfaris and "Surf Rider" by The Lively Ones and thousands of other songs by bands who had a glorious moment or two in the sun and then were never heard from again.

* * *

Instrumental surf music came first, but vocal surf wasn't far behind. The Beach Boys became so dominant that Brian Wilson could hand off unused songs to Jan and Dean: "Surf City," with its enticing and entirely false promise: "Two girls for every boy." In a feverish 11-month stretch from October 1962 to September 1963, The Beach Boys made three albums—*Surfin' Safari*, *Surfin' U.S.A.* and *Surfer Girl*—bursting with surf songs. But then they quickly switched gears—literally, in fact—to car songs like "Little Deuce Coupe" and "Fun, Fun, Fun," which didn't require much adjustment beyond slightly less reverb.

You could say that surf music died out pretty quickly after that, especially as four lads from Liverpool pretty much killed all-instrumental rock 'n' roll, spurring Brian Wilson to get bolder and weirder. By the time "Wipe Out" had its second run into the Top 20 in 1966, stars like Dick Dale were off the charts and on to the oldies circuit. But really, surf didn't die so much as morph from a genre to an ethos: a universally understood sense of fun in the sun that underpinned everything from "California Sun" to "California Dreamin' " to the sadder Beach Boys songs like "Caroline, No" and "Surf's Up," whose melancholy drew resonance from the frivolity and joy of those earlier songs.

Real surfers, meanwhile, began to stake their own claim on the surf-movie genre, not as mindless escapism but as adventure documentary. Surf docs had been a thing since Bud Browne started making them in the 1940s, but the watershed was Bruce Brown's *The Endless Summer* in 1966, which made the surf movie an event for its own community rather than an entertainment for people who'd never get on a board. The late author Eve Babitz chronicled the Santa Monica Civic Auditorium premiere of Greg MacGillivray and Jim Freeman's 1972 film *Five Summer Stories* this way:

> *A sudden roar rose up from the audience as the movie came fearlessly onscreen with some trance-imposing abstract colors, solarized colors in slow, slow motion turning slowly, dragging us into its rhythms and gutting us into awed silence before the whole thing changed into realer and realer color and at last was bright, blazing*

truth—a man sliding down the inside of a 15-foot sheet of molten
green with diamonds shooting out at the top and as the wave curled
lazily into itself the man drew back into the loop of air inside—the
"tube"—and vanished until, at the last moment, the final moment,
he pulled back out into the open. We cheered our devotion.

Half a century later, those cheers reverberate. Even when surf
music, surf movies, surf culture fade from the forefront, they lurk
beneath the surface.

* * *

At one point while I was writing this, my wife and I drove up the
California coast for a short vacation, stopping for two days in the
seaside town of Cambria. Our hotel was just across a small road from
Moonstone Beach, a stretch of sand that is about as far as you can
get [in some ways, if not geographically] from Malibu. The beach is
covered with small stones until you get right to the water's edge; the
water is much colder than it is down south and a chilly breeze often
comes in off the ocean. The waves are known to be consistent there,
but they didn't look like much on this particular late-April morning as
I peered from the hotel balcony through the morning fog. But there
were surfers out there in the cold—a handful of black dots in the gray
water at first, then more than a dozen spread out across the small
expanse, bobbing and retreating and looking for swells worth the ride.

Most of them, no doubt, weren't yet born when Brian Wilson
started writing his songs 60 years earlier, or when Frankie and Annette
were a thing, or when surf documentaries drew crowds to auditoriums
in beach towns up and down the coast. Maybe they were children of the
surf punks, or maybe they'd just succumbed to something that exists
in the air, in the water, in the culture. Who knows? It's California. The
waves, of all kinds, keep coming.

STEVE POND is the author of *The Big Show: High Times and Dirty Dealings
Backstage at the Academy Awards* and a veteran music, film, television and
entertainment journalist for publications including *Rolling Stone* and the *Los
Angeles Times*.

THE OUTLIER BEACH

Written by **LILY HOÀNG** | **WHEN I FIRST MOVED** to San Diego, I specifically requested that my dates show me something impressive about my new city. The first guy took me to the San Diego Zoo. Another to Balboa Park. And then Sebastian offered me a sunset.

We met, as he'd suggested, in the parking lot for the Torrey Pines Gliderport. Because I hadn't been there before, I was looking for a parking lot. You know—something lined, something paved. Because I was going to watch the sunset, I wore a summer dress and sandals. Although not fancy, the sandals were made for my particular feet by a cobbler in Rome, purchased for just twenty euros. I have great sentimentality for them. All of this is to say: I was unprepared.

The date itself was fine, don't worry. I already gave him a name— and in the first paragraph too!

Following the directions on my phone, I turned into a dirt expanse and arrived at my destination. Sebastian found me quickly, and we swapped introductory remarks, and then I saw the Pacific. Not like it was the first time I'd seen it or anything, but the ocean is profound, every single time. Its majesty and enormity stun. And, of course, its capacity to exact domination over you—to injure or to kill—with neither effort nor guilt to persuade it otherwise. Romantic poets and philosophers cite the ocean as an example of the sublime. What other word could be used to more perfectly describe the complexity of awe felt when facing the ocean? Except—the ocean was pretty far away. Maybe in distance, measured horizontally, not so far away, but we were standing on the top of a bluff, and the ocean was way down at the bottom.

To our right, I watched the wind billow open a parachute, and two people flew right off the cliff's edge. When asked what superpower I would choose, I have never said flight. [Years later, when my youngest nephew visits me, we will make sure all the clasps are secure, and we, too, will fly.] Shortly thereafter, a hang glider queued up.

"How much of an adventure do you want to have to get to the ocean?" Sebastian asked. Recognizing the test, I demurred, "Well, I won't parachute down." The thing is: I didn't mean it. I did mean that under no circumstance would I parachute down—for one, it wasn't such a great height; a parachute would hardly function—and much more importantly, my preference would be for an escalator or an elevator to get me oceanside. Besides, I was dressed for a date, not a weekend hike. Of course, I said none of this. But, my not-so-clever [not even funny!] response returned the power of decision-making to him, and even though he was a complete stranger, I knew for a fact that we were not riding an escalator to get down to the ocean. "Yeah, well ..." He scratched at his head. "The truth is that one way is only a little bit easier." [To date, I have taken three different routes to get down to Black's Beach: the Saigon Trail; walking north from La Jolla Shores during low tide; and the steps down from the gliderport. The gliderport route is the most efficient, although it does require a small degree of dexterity and stamina. The city does not maintain any path down to Black's Beach. Rather than allow it to fall to disrepair, faithful devotees, a group that calls themselves the Black's Beach Bares, take care of the route from the gliderport down to the sand. I know there's a fourth way, which the internet tells me is accessible for UC San Diego students only. My faculty ID should work, but I prefer just knowing that a super-secret path exists. I don't want to ruin the secret. And also, Sebastian was factually incorrect: one way is not only a little bit easier but a lot.]

And so, we descended. Down and down some more. Three hundred feet of down. The leather of my sandals bit into my ankles, and the sand was unpredictably slippery. Along the way, Sebastian explained that Black's Beach is one of only a handful of nude beaches in the country and he hoped that I was comfortable with that. Buoyant and boyish, he said he really should've checked with me before we began, and he had meant to, he really had, but he forgot. It's likely that he tried some cheesy line on me then, about how meeting me had made him *et cetera*; the problem with being a writer and a professor of literature and single is that the language of dating is cliché. Romantic gestures, no matter how well-intentioned, are cliché. Sebastian promised me that the view was going to be worth my spilled sweat, and it was clear that we had very opposite estimations on how we thought the date was going.

The view, it turned out, was spectacular. With only a few more steps to descend, I unlooped my sandals and plunged my hot feet into the black sand. [Now about that sand: 1. Black's Beach is named for the family who once owned the land, not because the sand is black; 2. This is not the first black sand beach I'd been to. Years before, I went to Martinique with my friend Jackie, and a Caribbean man took us around his island to enjoy the different colored sand beaches there: white, black, and pink; 3. The black sand beach in Martinique was not named for the color of its sand either; 4. A black sand beach in the Bay Area is called Black Sands Beach; 5. Everyone knows black sand comes from volcanoes, but I haven't seen any volcanoes hanging out in San Diego. Have you?; 6. The sand at Black Sands Beach looks black because it came from either greywacke—a dark-colored sandstone— or some super old shale that got compressed during the tectonic hanky-panky of one continental and two oceanic plates meeting; 7. Those submarine canyons, just down there making these outrageous waves: A beach where you are discouraged from swimming, where's the joke?; and 8. The sand at Black's Beach is black because its source rock is primarily dark colored and lacking in silica, rich in iron, and heavier than your typical silica sand. And after an energetic wave pulls away that lighter silica sand, the stalwart black sand looks smashing.] Waves rolled and crashed, breaking. A few naked people walked around, and others reclined on towels, not unlike the non-naked people, who were also walking around or reclining on their towels. Surfers punctuated the ocean with vertical exclamations. The sun was plunging fast. It was a deep orange. William Herschel, discoverer of the planet Uranus, believed that sunspots appear when Solarians briefly lift the skirt of flames covering the surface of the sun to catch a quick glimpse at us, down here on Earth.

The hike up wasn't nearly as laborious as I'd anticipated, and Sebastian easily satisfied my request for something impressive in San Diego. We had a fun time together. Things ultimately didn't work out between us; if only I'd been warned to wear appropriate shoes, if only such an escalator existed to get us down to the ocean.

The nudity at Black's was unobtrusive to me that day, but then,

I was on a date. To anyone else on that beach, I was already coupled, happily so, it would seem, and therefore my womanliness was irrelevant. The next time I went to Black's, I hiked down with my friend Sabrina. We brought a whole picnic, and I was excited for time with my friend. The older, naked men were not vultures, per se, nor were they sharks, but they paraded their naked bodies in front of us, flaunting their bellies and everything else.

Periodically, one of these older naked men would assert himself into our conversation. We didn't remove a single item of clothing. Despite the interruptions, though, we left smiling and happy and satisfied. Most likely, we were still high from first the descent down, and then the ascent back up the cliff's face. But even without all those endorphins, Black's Beach is resplendence made manifest—a beauty that eyes alone cannot adequately absorb, a valenced wildness that is magnified and felt, transferred from its surface and its depth into mine.

LILY HOÀNG is the author of several books, including the novel *Underneath* and the essay collection *A Bestiary*. She is a professor of creative writing at the University of California San Diego.

MALIBU

Written by **MATT WARSHAW**

Originally published in Los Angeles Magazine, 1994

THE 1967 MALIBU INVITATIONAL SURFING CONTEST was the second biggest event of the summer, right behind the U.S. Championships. Ranking members of the *Surfer Magazine* staff settled into position like Roman Senators across the Malibu beachfront VIP area. Not one bit embarrassed by its "Bible of the sport" epithet, Surfer was leaning hard against the winds of change. The publisher had taken up golf and joined an Orange County country club. Editorials spelled out on the dangers of pot smoking. Bill Cleary, a staff writer, looked hopefully to a future in which surfing had passed through its "willy-nilly adolescence," and gained acceptance as a serious sport, with top riders competing in the Olympics. Strictly Establishment, in other words. Two years later, the magazine would execute a full whipturn in editorial policy and become one with the counterculture, with articles titles like "Hallucinations" and "Bells Beach Boogie," and a particularly memorable piece of contest coverage, in 1970, made up of a single, stream-of-consciousness sentence, five pages long.

But 1970 was worlds away from 1967, when all actions were piously judged by Surfer according to what was "good for the sport." Competition, organization, responsibility—these were good. What was bad, at least on that particular summer afternoon, was Miki Dora.

Dora was 32 years old in 1967. Known as "Mr. Malibu," erstwhile contemporary of Gidget, Kahuna and Moondoggie, a stylistic original, showman and scammer, intelligent and cunning, Dora had been fencing with *Surfer* and the "fascist ruling faction" for years. Bill Cleary, Dora wrote, was "one of the great frauds of our times." The Malibu Contest judges were "fat and out of shape," and he'd entered the event "for the sheer pleasure of shaking up the status quo."

Dora paddled out for his semifinal heat in mediocre, late-afternoon conditions, and rode three waves without incident. On his fourth wave, he got to his feet, angled toward the pier, trimmed high and stepped forward, where he dropped his trunks, bent over and served up a classic moon, letting *Surfer Magazine*, the judges, local dignitaries, and 1,000-plus spectators know just what he thought of organized surfing.

It was Dora's last contest. It was Malibu's last great moment.

"It's been dead for at least 15 years, and now it's starting to stink!" John Orlando's 1975 comment on Malibu's demise has become something of a surf-world classic, but it's difficult to really pinpoint when Malibu was sacked. Or if it's been sacked at all.

It is easy to see, though, that Malibu's spirit, in 1994, has fallen on hard times. It's nearly impossible, standing on the beach side of Pacific Coast Highway at Malibu Surfrider Beach, to gain a sense of history; to remember that from the end of World War II to the Summer of Love this was the center of the surfing world, crucible for a new way of life, and point of origin for a set of industries whose total gross is now in the tens of billions. The view today from PCH is pedestrian, not tragic: the whole scene gently awash in nostalgia and sentimentality and polluted water from the nearby Malibu Lagoon, and packed full of middle-aged surfers carefully re-creating Kennedy-era moves on "modern" longboards, hanging ten and kick-stalling, as predictable as the KRLA playlist. Some contemporary surfing takes place on the fringes, but nothing of note. Boundaries for the once-almighty Pit—a room-sized plot of sand at the bottom of the point, one-time base of operations for Malibu heavies; more selective than any House of Lords—have vanished under the towels and beer coolers of visitors from Tarzana, Thousand Oaks and Van Nuys.

You need to back away from the here and now to get perspective. Just how big is the story of Malibu surfing? Sam George, veteran surf journalist, takes no prisoners: "Malibu not only defined surfing, it defined California. Before Malibu, there wasn't a real California style. Farming and aerospace? So what? Hollywood? Transplant New Yorkers; everyone knows that. But after the war, when the guys came home, and they'd done their bit for their country, and now they just wanted to relax—they went surfing. They hung out on the beach.

Then came *Gidget* and the Beach Boys, and the California scene was happening. Tab Hunter and Robert Redford? You want to know why people suddenly liked those handsome, blonde guys? Because they looked like the dudes hanging out at the Pit at Malibu."

Ten years before Dora's breech exit from competition, surfing and Malibu had already defined one another. Allowing for exceptions, it can be said that every development in equipment and technique, from multi-finned surfboards to the roundhouse cutback, can be traced back to Malibu; that all surfers in the world today have taken on, part or parcel, the values, attitude, humor and style first developed at Malibu; and that every surfing outpost, from the surf shop in Tel Aviv, to the professional contest in Vietnam, to surf expeditions into outer Sumatra, the Gulf of Alaska and southern China, can, with a little bit of creative thinking, be seen as Malibu colonization. Malibu surfing—defined by a rock-solid set of iconographic images, including the "perfect wave," sun and sand, babes on the beach [chicks and dudes], and the surfer-as-rebel—dropped like a piano into the wading pool of popular culture in the late '50s. It's impossible to gauge exactly Malibu surfing's collective impact on the world, but any measurement has to include national [even international] adaptation of "dude," "bitchin," "scarf," and "dweeb"; grand openings for surf generating "wavepools" in Tokyo, Tempe, Allentown and Edmonton; and units of clothing sold by Ocean Pacific, Quiksilver, Hang Ten, Gotcha, Billabong, Stussy, Maui and Sons.

On top of that, factor in the number of times Malibu has served as a backdrop for the rich, famous, powerful and beautiful: Peter Lawford, Jackie Coogan and Cliff Robertson, for instance, surfing First Point in the '40s and '50s. Or J. Paul Getty's confessional, just before his death in 1976, that the only happiness he ever knew was riding Malibu as a young man. Or local boy Dave Rochlen working out of his girlfriend "Honeybear" Warren's garage in 1947, with full approval of her Dad, the Governor, shaping a redwood board for Gary Cooper. Or [predictably] President Kennedy and Marilyn Monroe, in 1961, poorly disguised in hats and dark glasses, walking up the Point for an afternoon tryst in the Colony.

Real Malibu surfers, beginning with the "surfin' craze" period of the late-'50s and early '60s, were ambivalent about the big, sloppy mainstream embrace. Extra work in films, for a lucky few, paid up to

$150 a day. And, more subtly, along with the national interest came a kind of lifestyle validation. On the other hand, everyone knew that the entertainment/fashion conglomerate was a nation of non-surfers, and that, to one degree or another, they were screwing it up. By the time the Beach Boys' "Surfin'" hit the charts, in January, 1962, Malibu was being smothered. On a hot summer day, with a 4' south swell running, as many as 200 surfers might be floating around the line-up, with a like number reclined on the beach. Maybe not dead, as John Orlando would say 13 years later, but certainly feverish.

Malibu's sand and rock point measures about 400 yards from the pier to the mouth of Malibu lagoon, and actually contains three partially-connected surf breaks; First Point, Second Point and Third Point. All three break best during late summer and early fall, when Pacific storms between Baja and New Zealand generate south swells. Unlike the Gothic winter surf in Hawaii, defined by power, fear and conquest, the waves at Malibu, as they roll from the top of the point down toward the pier, rarely more than 6' high, are refined and precise, smooth, rounded, and gently tapered—almost Art Deco. The original perfect wave. "It goes along at a medium-to-fast speed," says Craig Styck, artist/writer and unofficial Malibu historian, "and it's a neutral medium. You can cruise, and that's fine. Or you can push as hard as you want, and it'll match you."

The surf was just the beginning. Terry Tracey—Maximum Leader of the Pit in the late '50s, aka the Kahuna, aka Tubesteak—thinks about the general Malibu ambiance for a moment and says, with charming seriousness: "Remember how, when Tinkerbell flies, all those sparkles came down behind her, all the magic sparkles?" The fingers on Tubesteak's sun-mottled, 59-year-old hands rise up and flutter slowly downward. "Malibu was just covered with that stuff."

Malibu is only slightly greater than the sum of its parts; the pleasing curve of the beach, the warm sand, the blue Pacific and the rolling hills, all bathed in what writer Carey McWilliams called the "miraculous" California light. "It has no counterpart in the world," McWilliams wrote in the mid-'40s. "Let the light turn soft with ocean mist [and] the most commonplace objects assume a matchless perfection of form."

Tubesteak, supportive of his Tinkerbell illustration, recalls a late summer afternoon when the surf was almost nonexistent. The sun had just set, the ocean was warm amber, two or three beach umbrellas were still in the sand, and tiny, crystalline waves broke across the point, as the first few pinpoints of light began shining out from the buildings of Santa Monica. "No other place in the world," Tubesteak finishes, "has that kind of feel."

As far as we know, Malibu was surfed for the first time in 1927, by Tom Blake, a 23-year-old vegetarian and national swimming champion, originally from Milwaukee, who had moved to Los Angeles in 1921. In 1926, Blake designed and built the first semi-hollow surfboard/paddleboard, streamlining a solid "plank" redwood board, drilling hundreds of holes through the deck, then covering the top and bottom with a thin sheet of veneer. Blake's new board was 16' long and weighed about 110 pounds; later versions, chambered instead of drilled, soon known as "cigar box" boards, would be lighter.

THE SUN HAD JUST SET, THE OCEAN WAS WARM AMBER, BEACH UMBRELLAS WERE STILL IN THE SAND. TINY WAVES BROKE ACROSS THE POINT.

In September of 1927, Blake and Sam Reid slid their boards into the rumble seat of Blake's Ford and drove up the coast, past the western border of Rancho Malibu, parked at the Los Flores gate, got out, stripped down, muscled their boards to the water, and began paddling north.

It was a symbolic moment. Almost everybody in Southern California wanted access to Rancho Malibu. Proprietor Rhoda May Knight Rindge, the imperious "Queen of the Malibu" as labeled by the grossly politicized Los Angeles press, had fought for 25 years, legally and extralegally, to block public access across her 17,000-acre domain, the last intact Spanish land grant, which stretched along 26 miles of coast, from Topanga to Arroyo Sequit. The Supreme Court ruled against her in 1923. The Roosevelt Highway, later renamed Pacific Coast Highway, opened in 1929, and Mrs Rindge, broke, was forced to subdivide an attractive strip of land just north of Malibu Point. Beachfront lots sold for $2,600. Bing Crosby, Clara Bow, Barbara Stanwyck and Gary Cooper were among the first to buy, and the

Malibu Movie Colony was born.

Back in the water, Blake and Reid, trespassers, paddled into a modest wave and rode side by side down the point, holding a steady line all the way to the cove, where the two surfers, in unison, stepped from their boards to the sand. Just by riding hollow boards and holding a tight angle along the unbroken face of the wave, at a time when the rest of the surfers in the state [perhaps numbering 100] rode planks and aimed straight for the beach, Blake and Reid had left everyone else in the dust. Standards in equipment and technique would be set and reset at Malibu for the next 40 years.

The post-War years were nearly frantic with change, as Bob Simmons, Joe Quigg, Dale Velzy and Matt Kivlin, from 1946 to 1950, bounced theory and design off one another like nuclear physicists on vacation from Los Alamos. Blake's "cigar-box" boards were discarded; the new boards were thinned-out balsa or redwood-balsa-pine laminates, with a fiberglass and resin shell. There was experimentation with multi-finned boards, rope handles, "spoon" noses, concave bottoms, rolled bottoms, split-level bottoms, Styrofoam and plywood laminates, pintails and swallowtails. Board size dropped as low as 8'.

Quigg made an extra-light 60-pound board for Darrylin Zanuck [daughter of proto-mogul Darryl Zanuck] in July of 1947, and, after a collective decision that masculinity wouldn't be compromised by riding a "girls board," Dave Rochlen and Tommy Zahn, two of Malibu's best surfers, semi-permanently borrowed Zanuck's board. Three years later, Quigg made a 24-pounder for his wife, Aggie. The alpha-males, again, moved in. From that point on, the lightweight "Malibu chip" board became standard-issue.

Performance kept up with changes in design. The straight line was being bent, if not yet broken. Kivlin and Les Williams, in particular, were finding a whole new range of motion using the new equipment. "It was a type of high-performance totally alien to California surfing as it then existed," wrote Craig Stecyk in 1992. "It was pocket surfing and nose riding, and turning sharply around the curl, in contrast to the more gentlemanly angling practiced elsewhere along the coast."

At this point, too, crowds came into play for the first time. For more than 20 years, there had been plenty for all. Tom Blake, Sam Reid and a dozen others surfed Malibu during the Depression, with perhaps 3-4 surfers in the water on any given summer afternoon.

During the war, of course, Malibu was empty. Or almost empty. LeRoy Grannis, 76, remembers how the Coast Guard commandeered the entire point at Malibu and had recruits marching up and down the shoreline, on guard against the Japanese mini-sub invasion, expected at any moment. LeRoy's brother, Don, was stationed at Malibu and had an eight-hour night patrol. After his shift, he'd surf by himself, then drag his board up to the barracks on the point and crash. "I got out of the service myself in September of '45," recalls LeRoy, "got back to Malibu in early October, and there were maybe fifteen guys in the water. Fifteen guys! I turned to my buddy and said, 'Well, that's it. Malibu's ruined.'"

By the early '50s, Malibu was established as the center of the surf universe. The once-great Palos Verdes Cove crew had peaked in the interwar years. The San Onofre brotherhood, grown complacent on Sano's easy, puffball surf, were already known as old-timers. True, the most progressive surfer in the world was Rabbit Kekai from Honolulu, but the Malibu boys, having visited the Islands in Spring of '50, were hip to Kekai's approach long before anyone else on the coast.

The only other energetic spot in California was La Jolla's Windansea. Comparative discussion between Malibu and La Jolla, however, isn't worth Tubesteak's time. "Hey, listen. you think anybody would've gone to see *Gidget Goes to Windansea*? Come on. The La Jolla guys were little league. They were T-ball. Malibu was the Majors."

By 1957, there were 70, 80, even 100 surfers out at Malibu at the same time. "Well, there you go," Tubesteak says with a sigh and a shrug. "Everybody wants to be in the Majors."

"In the early years of my surfing," says Billy Hamilton, one of the premier surf stylists of the '60s and early '70s, "when I was still trying to figure out how to hold my arms and hands, I was thumbing through the Bible and came across a picture of Jesus giving the Sermon on the Mount, and he's standing there, with his hands up a certain way, and I thought to myself, 'Hey, that would look bitchin' for a cutback.'"

Style is tremendously important to surfing, because the act never did and never will cut it as objective sport. "Style," says Phil Edwards, "really is the whole point of surfing." And true mastery, as Hamilton and Edwards both know, goes well beyond arm and finger positioning, or proper hip-and-shoulder rotation, or maintaining composure from deep inside the vortex of a massive Pipeline cylinder, into a wider realm of general conduct.

Modern surfer style, unlike surfing itself, isn't even remotely connected to ancient Polynesia, where riding waves was both commonplace and noble, and thoroughly understood by the community. Surfing's character, as it exists today, is a local product, created between 1907, when Henry Huntington brought 24-year-old Irish-Hawaiian surfer George Freeth over from Waikiki as an "aquatic attraction" for the Redondo-Los Angeles Railway, and 1959, when Tubesteak decided to pack it in after the Los Angeles County lifeguards deposed him as ruler of Malibu point.

From '59 into the early '60s, as the surfin' craze tipped California on its side and displaced tens of thousands of teenagers from their tract-house neighborhoods, depositing them as gremmie larvae on nearby beaches, the ultimate Malibu character—and, therefore, it might be said, the ultimate surfing character—went into his final stages of development. "Dora was it," Tubesteak says today. "You wouldn't trust him further than you could throw him. But there was a time when you'd walk down the Point at Malibu and everybody, I mean everybody, was copying him. His surfing, of course. But also the way he moved his hands, combed his hair, the way he talked, everything."

Discussion continues about whether Miki Dora or Phil Edwards was the greatest surfer of the late '50s and early '60s. Edwards was big and indestructible, well-rounded, hugely talented, but in a comprehendible way. Dora's approach was enigmatic and sly. He rode in a casual slouch, maneuvering with his ankles, breaking trim with endless, quirky adjustments, while his hands moved in stylized patterns, almost like a flamenco dancer. The end result was sophisticated and slightly manic.

But his reputation went far beyond physical talent. He was surfing's great anti-hero; bigger, within his own sphere, than Kerouac or Kowalski; idolized by thousands who needed a rebel-king; hated by lifeguards, contest organizers, and authority figures of all stripes. By the early '60s, Dora's interests had graduated from pranks [releasing a satchel full of moths during the screening of a surf flick] and hazing of Malibu gremmies [stealing a kid's board, returning it after two or three days of abject grovelling], to the surf media and surf politics. Magazine articles by or about Dora turned up like letter bombs in the surf press, critical and humorous, paranoia running like an undertow beneath each sentence—something like Hunter Thompson's West Coast doppelganger. But Dora's time at Malibu, by the late '60s, was coming to a close. Standards were changing: the best surfers in the world were Australian or Hawaiian. The North Shore of Oahu had replaced Malibu as surfing's performance center. And as Tubesteak always said, if you want to be a surf legend, don't hang around too long.

Dora left California in 1970, wanted by the police for check fraud and failure to appear on a small number of trespass and driving violations—a relatively innocuous rap sheet which, a few years later, with Dora still out of the country, would be magnified and distorted into a legend of high-finance swindling and international espionage. Dora's stature grew as the years passed. Occasionally he'd be seen riding waves in France, Mexico, South America, South Africa.

Dora's kiss-off to Malibu, following the '67 contest, was bitter and slightly poignant. "I remember how things were before the subdividers, concessionaires and lifeguards—before exploiters polluted the beaches like they do everything else. You can have the place. The water's curdling already from the football-punchy Valley swingers, surf dopes, magazine and photo hacks, and lapdog surf star club rah-rah boys; the same old story, year after year. I hope you all become one while stewing in your own juices. For myself, I'm dropping out."

The Malibu experience for Tom Blake, Dale Velzy, Kathy Kohner and Miki Dora was predicated on being involved with something that the rest of the world hadn't yet caught on to. Today, a degree of concentration is needed to remember that the laid-back, sun-baked, Southern Californian beach approach, now one of the great American clichés, was, in years long past, not just totally bitchin', but totally new and different. In a way, Malibu is now more an idea than a place. The present is tolerated, the past is revered: surfing's version of Deism, with Malibu, the Creator, alive in spirit only. On the right day, with the right wave, however, that spirit can still move through you.

MATT WARSHAW is the executive director of The Encyclopedia of Surfing, a nonprofit website on surf history and culture. His books include *The History of Surfing*, and *Mavericks: The Story of Big-Wave Surfing*. A Los Angeles native and former pro surfer, Warshaw now lives in Seattle, Washington.

DIRECTORY
& INDEX